BONHOEFFER

OUTSTANDING CHRISTIAN THINKERS

Series Editor: Brian Davies OP, Professor of Philosophy at Fordham University, New York.

The Cappadocians
Anthony Meredith SJ

Augustine
Mary T. Clark RSCJ

Catherine of Siena
Giuliana Cavallini OP

Kierkegaard
Julia Watkin

Lonergan
Frederick Rowe SJ

Reinhold Niebuhr
Kenneth Durkin

The Venerable Bede
Benedicta Ward SLG

The Apostolic Fathers
Simon Tugwell OP

Denys the Areopagite
Andrew Louth

Calvin
T. H. L. Parker

Hans Urs von Balthasar
John O'Donnell SJ

Teresa of Avila
Archbishop Rowan Williams

Bultmann
David Fergusson

Karl Barth
John Webster

Aquinas
Brian Davies OP

Paul Tillich
John Heywood Thomas

Karl Rahner
William V. Dych SJ

Anselm
G. R. Evans

Newman
Avery Cardinal Dulles SJ

Bonhoeffer
Stephen Plant

BONHOEFFER

Stephen Plant

continuum
LONDON • NEW YORK

Continuum

The Tower Building
11 York Road
London SE1 7NX

15 East 26 Street
New York
NY 10010

www.continuumbooks.com

First published 2004

British Library Cataloguing-in-Publication Data
A catalogue record for this book is available from the British Library.

ISBN 0 8264 5088 1 (hardback)
ISBN 0 8264 5089 X (paperback)

Typeset by Fakenham Photosetting Ltd, Fakenham, Norfolk NR21 8NN
Printed and bound by MPG Books Ltd, Bodmin, Cornwall

Contents

Editorial Foreword

St Anselm of Canterbury (1033–1109) once described himself as someone with faith seeking understanding. In words addressed to God he says 'I long to understand in some degree thy truth, which my heart believes and loves. For I do not seek to understand that I may believe, but believe in order to understand.'

This is what Christians have always inevitably said, either explicitly or implicitly. Christianity rests on faith, but it also has content. It teaches and proclaims a distinctive and challenging view of reality. It naturally encourages reflection. It is something to think about; something about which one might even have second thoughts.

But what have the greatest Christian thinkers said? And is it worth saying? Does it engage with modern problems? Does it provide us with a vision to live by? Does it make sense? Can it be preached? Is it believable?

The Outstanding Christian Thinkers series is offered to readers with questions like these in mind. It aims to provide clear, authoritative and critical accounts of outstanding Christian writers from New Testament times to the present. It ranges across the full spectrum of Christian thought to include Catholic and Protestant thinkers, thinkers from East and West, thinkers ancient, medieval and modern.

The series draws on the best scholarship currently available, so it will interest all with a professional concern for the history of Christian ideas. But contributors also write for general readers who have little or no previous knowledge of the subjects to be dealt with. Its volumes should therefore prove helpful at a popular as well as an academic level. For the most part they are devoted to a single thinker, but occasionally the subject is a movement or school of thought.

Brian Davies OP

For
Catherine James (née Holland)
1963–2001

Preface

Dietrich Bonhoeffer is one of the best-known theologians of the twentieth century but not often the best understood. Few theologians, of any century, are burdened by his celebrity status. His life-story has been told in half a dozen biographies, in documentaries, films, comic strips and operas; there is even a Bonhoeffer rock musical. Since his death, Bonhoeffer's writings have been press-ganged into authorizing astonishingly varied theological and ethical positions. A full bibliography of books and articles about Bonhoeffer sprawls across hundreds of pages. Why add more?

The publication of a complete scholarly edition of Bonhoeffer's books, sermons, papers and letters in German, and the steady translation of the German original into the *Dietrich Bonhoeffer Works*, has made the raw materials for the study of Bonhoeffer more accessible than ever before. Tools and materials that were formerly unavailable to all but the most determined researcher are now collected in a standard edition, cross-referenced and footnoted, and are being translated into consistent English texts. A revised English edition of Eberhard Bethge's magisterial *Dietrich Bonhoeffer: A Biography* was published in 2000. But these new resources alone cannot account for the recent resurgence of interest in Bonhoeffer in churches and amongst students. Christians confront difficult questions at the beginning of the third Millennium and we are discovering that some of the avenues opened up by twentieth-century theology lead to dead ends. Not all of Dietrich Bonhoeffer's theology is equally helpful but enough of it points forward to make him a good companion and guide on the Christian journey. He was and is an outstanding Christian thinker.

This book tries to do three things. Firstly and most importantly, it aims to *introduce* Bonhoeffer and his theology. Because this book is an introduction I have used endnotes only where omitting them commits plagiarism, or where they help make connections a reader might want to follow up. The book avoids lengthy engagement with secondary literature about Bonhoeffer's life and theology in order to pay full attention to Bonhoeffer's own writings. In a longer book I would have made more use of Bonhoeffer's less well known theological writings, as well as of his correspondence and papers, but in what follows I have focused primarily on Bonhoeffer's key writings. I have tried to keep things simple: Bonhoeffer was right to comment that 'simplicity is an intellectual achievement, one of the greatest' (*LPP* 385). Yet complex subjects are also ill served by over-simplification and I have not avoided Bonhoeffer's more difficult ideas. I have tried not to make assumptions about how much you, as reader, know about Bonhoeffer's life or theology, or about history and theology in general. But I do make one significant assumption: that theology does not exist for its own sake, but to serve God's Church. In the introduction to a late volume of his *Church Dogmatics*, Karl Barth (whose name features prominently in what follows) noted that many of his contemporaries who had laboured for forty years in pastoral ministry were now retiring. 'For three decades' Barth wrote 'I have no longer been taking any direct share in this work. But what I have done in the meantime has been intended for its benefit.' It is ridiculous to compare the purposes of this book to those of Barth's *Dogmatics*, but his wistful dedication does remind us that theology must keep its eyes fixed on the needs of the Church and the world. Theology, as Bonhoeffer puts it, 'arises from those on bended knees'. It is for this reason that I have, from time to time, made connections between Bonhoeffer's theology and issues confronting Christians today.

A second aim in this book, further than introducing Bonhoeffer's life and thought, is to set Bonhoeffer in his social, historical and intellectual *context*. Bonhoeffer's writing only makes sense if read against the events through which he lived because as much as for any theologian, his life and theology are inextricably intertwined. English-speaking readers typically know little of the history of Germany in the twentieth century into which I set Bonhoeffer's biography in Chapter 2. Similarly, most of those educated outside Germany do not understand the extent of Bonhoeffer's indebtedness to certain key figures in German philosophy and theology. Some English-speaking readers have consequently misunderstood what Bonhoeffer means, or have attributed ideas to him that actually originate with his sources. In Chapter 3, I therefore try to give an idea of how several key thinkers mark his thought. Only then will I begin to explore Bonhoeffer's theology, before evaluating Bonhoeffer's theological ethics in the concluding chapter.

A third aim in this book is to suggest a means by which the *consistencies* in Bonhoeffer's theology can be brought into the open. Aside from his early academic career, Bonhoeffer's theology emerged in emergency situations, often under pressures of time, as well as of urgency and danger. His writings come to us in frustratingly fragmentary forms; lectures pieced together from student notes, barely decipherable manuscripts on poor quality paper; fragments imperfectly arranged into books and letters smuggled from prison. Honestly, all this adds to the 'romance' of reading Bonhoeffer, but it has made it more difficult to discern anything resembling a coherent 'Bonhoefferian' theology. Does this perhaps explain why Bonhoeffer scholarship has relied unduly on the short essay, rather than the monograph: scrappy responses to a scrappy thinker? I think not; I believe that it is not only possible to uncover coherent patterns and trajectories in Bonhoeffer, but that it is important so to do. It is because I do not think that this is obvious that I have also set myself the task of making a case for it in what follows. And the coherence and consistency I hope to illuminate lies in considering Bonhoeffer as a theologian with a particular interest in ethics. Naturally, not everything he wrote can be viewed from an ethical perspective, but I suggest that his theology is a consistent, and by and large credible attempt to describe how people should live together and conduct themselves in the light of the Gospel of Jesus. My argument is not *the* hermeneutical key, a new 'aha' thesis that trumps all previous interpretations of Bonhoeffer; neither is this the first book to explore Bonhoeffer's ethics. Yet this book does, I hope, offer something new in tracking ethical questions and concerns from Bonhoeffer's earliest to his last writings. The Outstanding Christian Thinkers series, to which this volume contributes, does not permit a book to have a title other than the name of its subject; but were this book to have a title, because the theme of ethics is so prominent, it would probably be 'A silence on the cross: the theological ethics of Dietrich Bonhoeffer'.

Most books incur debts, and this one certainly does. I am grateful to Brian Davies OP for inviting me to write this book, and to the staff of Continuum for their patience as its deadlines came and went. The World Church Office of the Methodist Church in Britain funds the half of my post dedicated to research which makes writing possible. My thanks also go to the members of my support group at

Wesley House, to colleagues and students in the Cambridge Theological Federation and in Cambridge University; to Keith Clements, John de Gruchy, Matt Finch, David Ford, Clifford Green, Dan Hardy, David Horrell, John Kennedy, Joel Lawrence, Iain Murton, Nicholas Sagovsky and Simon Sutcliffe, in whose company theology becomes joyful. My wife Kirsty Smith, our son Caleb and the child we expect before this book is published, keep book-writing and study in their proper place and it would take another book to record all of my debts to them.

1

Introduction: 'a silence on the cross'

FRIDAY'S CHILD
(IN MEMORY OF DIETRICH BONHOEFFER,
MARTYRED AT FLOSSENBÜRG, APRIL 9TH, 1945)
W.H. Auden

He told us we were free to choose
But, children as we were, we thought –
'Paternal Love will only use
    Force in the last resort

On those too bumptious to repent' –
Accustomed to religious dread,
It never crossed our minds He meant
    Exactly what He said.

Perhaps He frowns, perhaps He grieves,
But it seems idle to discuss
If anger or compassion leaves
    The bigger bangs to us.

What reverence is rightly paid
To a Divinity so odd

He lets the Adam whom He made
    Perform the Acts of God?

It might be jolly if we felt
Awe at this Universal Man
(When kings were local, people knelt);
    Some try to, but who can?

The self-obsessed observing Mind
We meet when we observe at all
Is not alarming or unkind
    But utterly banal.

Though instruments at Its command
Make wish and counterwish come true,
It clearly cannot understand
    What It can clearly do.

Since the analogies are rot
Our senses based belief upon,
We have no means of learning what
    Is really going on,

And must put up with having learned
All proofs or disproofs that we tender
Of His existence are returned
    Unopened to the sender.

Now, did He really break the seal
And rise again? We dare not say;
But conscious unbelievers feel
    Quite sure of Judgement Day.

Meanwhile, a silence on the cross,
As dead as we will ever be,
Speaks of some total gain or loss,
    And you and I are free

To guess from the insulted face
Just what Appearances He saves
By suffering in a public place
    A death reserved for slaves.

? 1958

2

By the early 1960s Stephen Spender thought that there was no one from whom the poet W.H. Auden got anything new 'except perhaps a theologian'.[1] The late fifties and early sixties were an unhappy time in Auden's life and *Friday's Child*, dedicated to Bonhoeffer's memory, is one of the few fine poems he wrote during this period. At University Auden had abandoned Christianity, experimenting with what he would later call the 'Christian heresies' of Blake, Freud, Lawrence and Marx. But from 1939 he slipped gradually and inconspicuously back into the Church. At first, under the influence of Søren Kierkegaard's theology, he considered Christian faith in existentialist terms as a 'leap of faith'. But this jarred with his experience, which was of a slow, intellectual taking hold of God in which the act of faith remains an act of choice which no one can do for another. Auden read a good deal of theology – not only Augustine and Newman, staples of the Anglo-Catholic diet, but Schleiermacher, Bultmann, Barth and, it seems, Dietrich Bonhoeffer. 'I like to think', he told a friend 'that if I hadn't been a poet, I might have become an Anglican Bishop – politically liberal, I hope; theologically and liturgically conservative, I know'. W. H. Auden was born a year after Bonhoeffer, on 21 February 1907 but they had little in common. Both men fuelled their considerable intellectual faculties with tobacco, both admired Kierkegaard and Barth; but it is hard to imagine two more disparate individuals. In theory they could have met: Auden arrived in New York in January 1939, Bonhoeffer followed six months later. But they moved in very different circles and while Bonhoeffer promptly decided to return to Germany to share the fate of his nation, no amount of moral pressure could persuade Auden he had a responsibility to go home and contribute to his country's war effort, however trivially.

Auden discovered Bonhoeffer's theology relatively early, at any rate before Bishop J. A. T. Robinson's controversial book *Honest To God* popularized Bonhoeffer for the 1960s' generation of radical theologians. *Friday's Child* was published at Christmas, 1958. The poem is not necessarily a rendering of Auden's faith, nor a commentary on Bonhoeffer's theology; still less is it a eulogy over the dead theologian's unmarked grave. Its significance for our purposes is that *Friday's Child* organizes poetically a theological dilemma that is key to Bonhoeffer's thought. It is a dilemma that begins with the freedom to choose and ends with the silence of the cross. Poets, Auden thought, interpret theology in a rather unique way because in poetry myth and dogma are fused together. Without directly expositing Bonhoeffer's theological ethics *Friday's Child*

3

dissolves them instinctively in the Christian images of Judgement Day, cross and resurrection. The phrase 'Friday's child' is from a nursery rhyme, and Auden's poem retains its childlike cadencies. Christ is Friday's child, characterized in the rhyme as 'loving and giving'; what He gives is freedom to choose belief or unbelief, obedience or disobedience. Whether it is God's anger or His compassion that provides the explanation, God leaves 'the bigger bangs' – the bigger choices – 'to us'. Just this donation of free responsibility is, Auden suggests, the remarkable feature of the Christian Deity, who 'lets the Adam whom He made/Perform the Acts of God'. Auden understood that the Holocaust shattered older forms of religious belief that had in any case been eroding since the Enlightenment. Patterns of reverence, common 'when kings were local', have gone for good. The foundations on which we based our knowledge of God now seem shaky, such that 'We have no means of learning what/is really going on'. Faith and theology can no longer be a matter of apologetics, of proving or disproving the existence of God; such questions are simply 'returned/Unopened to the sender'. We live today, as Bonhoeffer put it in his prison letters, in a world 'as if God were not given'. And yet, confronted with the possibility of resurrection, even 'conscious unbelievers' can feel Judgement Day bearing upon them. In the last two stanzas of the poem Auden reaches the cross; here God is embodied, not in the frantic fruitlessness of metaphysical theology, but in a silence that speaks. On the cross we hear the 'total gain or loss' of Christ, which leaves us guessing:

> Just what Appearances He saves
> By suffering in a public place
>   A death reserved for slaves.

Christian ethics is lived out in this silence. Auden's *Friday's Child* intimates a performance of human life in the space God creates between freedom of choice and a silence on the cross. This freedom has nothing in common with the anarchic chaos of sexual revolution or mind-blowing drugs; neither does it resemble the often superficial and artificial freedoms of contemporary life. It is a freedom fastened to the utter self-giving of God in Christ Jesus. Put simply: God's silence on the cross signs our freedom as human beings to be responsible for our own choices, to create our own ethical life; this is made possible by the incarnation of God in the world. Jesus' death stills the clamour of ethics in 'a silence on the cross'; not the empty prattle of a godless world but the engaged, arcane silence of God in a world come of age.

I am suggesting that theological ethics are a central concern of Bonhoeffer's theology, but just what are *theological ethics*? We can all recognize a moral problem. On some moral issues almost everyone will agree. If I ask 'is lying right or wrong?' or 'if I disagree with a politician should I kill him?' or 'if I want a son and a pre-natal scan shows my foetus to be female, is it right to abort the pregnancy and try again?' most people will give the same answers. Yet moral questions are not always so clear-cut. If I ask 'is lying wrong when, by telling a lie I can prevent someone from being hurt?' or 'if a tyrant is killing thousands of people is it right to kill him?', or 'if a scan shows that my foetus has Down syndrome should I abort the pregnancy and try again?' then we can expect greater diversity in people's responses. Whatever conclusions we draw we recognize these sorts of questions as 'moral' or 'ethical'. But doing the right or wrong thing when faced with certain choices is only part of what morality or ethics are about. Our actions, taken collectively, have a lot to do with who we are, with our moral identity. This is why we often distinguish between good and bad people. Most people can agree that Hitler and Pol Pot were bad people and that Saint Francis and Gandhi were good people. Again, sometimes matters are less clear-cut: some people in Russia still admire Stalin, while others think that Mother Theresa would have done more good in Calcutta by distributing condoms than by caring for the dying. Dietrich Bonhoeffer too is morally controversial: to some a martyr and saint, to others a traitor and murderer. Thinking carefully about being good or bad is as much a part of morality and ethics as thinking about whether particular actions or choices are right or wrong.

'*Ethicos*' is a Greek word closely related to '*ethos*'. In classical Greek philosophy, 'ethicos' referred to issues of character, and also to custom, usage, manners or habit. Its first recorded use in English[2] is 1581 when it was used to mean 'relating to morals'. In English, the word 'ethos' is, in some respects, rather closer to the Greek original and is used in the sense of the prevailing tone or sentiment of a people, community or group, and the characteristic spirit of a system or institution. Relatively recently in English usage 'ethics' has come to refer to the science of moral philosophy or the moral system of a particular group or school of thought. '*Moralis*' is the Latin equivalent of '*ethicos*'. It derives from the plural form of '*mos/moris*', meaning nature, custom, practice or mood, as well as character and behaviour. The English word 'mores' retains a sense close to the Latin original. In English, 'moral' came to refer to the distinction between right and wrong in relation to specific actions. The German language also borrowed both '*ethik*' and '*moral*', but also has the words '*sittlich*' and '*sittlichkeit*' which, though usually translated 'moral' and 'morality', retain a more explicit connection to customs and mores than the English word 'moral' generally does.

Moral philosophers or ethicists have tended to conceive their discipline in three ways. Firstly, ethics may be a descriptive enquiry, either historical or scientific that seeks to account for moral actions, for example, anthropologically, psychologically, or sociologically. Secondly, ethics can refer to the attempt to develop normative patterns or rules for living. This might mean debating with one's self, or with others what to do or think in a specific situation. Finally, there is a much more self consciously 'philosophical' or 'academic' activity that reflects on patterns of moral activity in ways that are analytical or critical. This asks general logical, semantic or episte-mological (i.e. how we *know* anything ethically) questions such as 'what do we mean by the word "wrong" when we say "lying is wrong"'? or 'what kind of arguments would count logically as moral arguments if someone were to argue a moral case?', or 'what does it mean to be responsible?' Because this third kind of ethics takes place at a theoretical remove from the first two kinds, it is sometimes called 'meta-ethics'. Some ethical arguments will confine themselves to one of these three types; others will switch from one type to another. A convenient possibility is that we might use the term 'morality' to refer to the second of these types and 'ethics' to refer to the third, so that 'ethics' would mean the practice of reflecting on morality. Such a distinction is however, hard to maintain in practice, not only because the distinction is not normal in day-to-day conversation, but because it implies an over-sharp distinction between ethical theory and moral practice.

During the twentieth century, however, the ways people behave and the ways they reflect on moral issues, changed in most parts of the world to a greater or lesser extent. Whether in reaction to total-izing political ideologies such as Nazism, Fascism or Communism, or in the wake of the social disruption of two world wars, or under the influence of new philosophies such as existentialism or 'postmodernism', or with a decline in religious practice in some places, or in the light of scientific research into the extent human behaviour is determined by a genetic 'programme', or as seems likely, as a result of some combination of these and related factors, the neatness of the description of ethics outlined in the previous paragraph has come into question. Those who think a lot about moral issues have become more aware of how morally chaotic and confused the world has become. Some have tried to recover for the present a high point in the history of ethics represented, for example by Aristotle, Augustine or Aquinas; others have reflected on what it might mean to accept that people are shaped morally by very particular communities, such as families, churches and nations, instead of holding out for a 'universal ethics'; others have relished the confusion; others have simply accepted that moral behaviour is genetically determined and have essentially turned ethics into anthropology. Bonhoeffer's ethics are situated in the middle of many of these changes and if they are still to be of any use must contribute to moral reflection and practices in these new contexts.

Like everyone else, Christians make choices about what is right and wrong, and distinguish between good and bad people. And like moral philosophers, Christian theologians approach ethics in several ways. But whether or not Christian moral theology is the same as secular moral philosophy, and whether Christian theological ethics is identical with secular ethics is hotly disputed. On the one hand, some theologians argue that since Christians are human beings shaped by the same moral forces as everyone else, claiming that there is a separate Christian ethics amounts to no more than an ugly assertion of moral superiority. Richard Holloway's *Godless Morality: Keeping Religion out of Ethics*[3] makes just this case. Holloway argues that Christian ethics as a separate discipline should be done away with because claiming that Christian ways of behaving are sanctioned by God's commands merely asserts that Christian moral reasoning is divine while everyone else's is human. Since history teaches that many of the moral claims made by Christians have come subsequently to seem immoral, Holloway suggests that Christians would do well to show a little more humility and be a little less morally certain. Theologians like Stanley Hauerwas and Pope John Paul II articulate a very different view: they maintain that Christian ethics are quite distinct from the ethics that everyone else lives by. Typically, they believe, Christians maintain moral views that are at odds with those of the majority of non-Christians. Even when Christians come to the same moral conclusions as non-believers they do so for very different reasons. This is because secular ethics begins by asking 'what is the right thing to do?' while Christians begin by asking 'what does God want of me?' What this debate reveals is that in contemporary theology there is considerable uncertainty not only about what 'theological ethics' are – but about whether such a thing is possible at all.

Bonhoeffer understood the importance of these questions as well as anyone. The question 'is "Christian ethics" possible?' occupied Bonhoeffer's attention throughout his working life. In 1929, while serving as assistant minister to the German-speaking church in Barcelona, Bonhoeffer gave a lecture on 'Fundamental questions of a Christian ethic'. In 1931, at his first meeting with Karl Barth, they argued about the nature of ethics. During the summer semester of 1932 he led a seminar in Berlin University on the question 'Is there a Christian ethic?' In his doctoral dissertation on the Church, and in his books on discipleship and community life he explored the life of Christian communities, and the ways in which that life is distinct from other forms of human community. But it was during the war that Bonhoeffer paid greatest attention to ethics, preparing a book on the subject that was never completed. Reviewing his life from his prison cell in November 1943 Bonhoeffer wrote to Eberhard Bethge that though his ideas were incomplete 'I've reproached myself for not having finished my *Ethics* (parts of it have probably been confiscated), and it was some consolation to me that I had told you the essentials' (*LPP* 129). A month later he added 'I sometimes feel as if my life were more or less over, and as if all I had to do now were to finish my *Ethics*' (*LPP* 163). In a fragment for this unfinished book Bonhoeffer summed up his lifelong exploration of this key question:

> A Christian ethic will have to begin by asking whether and to what extent it is possible at all to treat the 'ethical' and the 'Christian' as a theme, for that is not by any means so self-evident as one might assume from the confidence with which this repeatedly has been and is being done. (*E* 231)

It is one thing to demonstrate that Bonhoeffer consistently questioned the nature of ethics; it is quite a different matter to demonstrate that he found an answer. Not everyone recognizes in Bonhoeffer, as Auden apparently did, an outstanding Christian thinker capable of doing more than simply asking the right questions. In May 1967 Karl Barth wrote to thank Eberhard Bethge for sending a copy of Bethge's recently published biography of Bonhoeffer.[4] In his 'expectorations' on the book Barth queried the value of Bonhoeffer's theology:

Wholly obscure to me, even after reading your book, is the matter on which discussion has raged from several angles since it was provoked by *Letters and Papers from Prison:* the renewal of theology in both the narrower and the broader sense as he envisioned it ... [T]o this day I do not know what Bonhoeffer himself meant and planned with it all, and very softly I venture to doubt whether theological systematics (I include his *Ethics*) was his real strength.

It was not that Barth casually disregarded what Bonhoeffer had written: his *Church Dogmatics* is salted with laudatory remarks about Bonhoeffer's early writings, which he had clearly read attentively. Barth's concern was that Bonhoeffer's was an 'agitated intellectual pilgrimage' curtailed by martyrdom before it had taken proper form. Today, some serious theologians with no desire to belittle Bonhoeffer's integrity are equally agnostic about whether or not his written legacy can be viewed as a coherent totality, whether there is a 'Bonhoefferian' theological ethics at all. Outside the claustrophobic circle of Bonhoeffer's most devoted admirers some theologians remain baffled that Bonhoeffer's ethics continue to be read when others' ethics are comparatively neglected.[5]

It is certainly the case that too much of Bonhoeffer's popularity rests on the mistaken view that the compelling story of his anti-Nazi resistance, ending on the gallows, serves to justify the quality of his theology. True, with Bonhoeffer biography and theology are interleaved; but many who have died bravely have thought unclearly. If Bonhoeffer is to speak to this new century as to the last then his theology must be capable of standing on its own feet. What we need to reveal is the way in which Bonhoeffer's theological ethics constitute a coherent whole; only on that basis can we assess their contribution to today's moral problems. By 'coherent' I do not mean a self-enclosed, complete system that contains all truth; Christian theology is not the kind of discipline that *can* be systematized, at any rate tidily or wisely. Revealing the coherence in Bonhoeffer's theological ethics will mean laying them out so that they make sense cumulatively; so that their beginning, middle and end hang together. I want to argue the case that a trajectory can be traced from Bonhoeffer's earliest to his final writings which describe an ethics of responsibility, lived out in obedience to the God who acts most powerfully in 'the silence of the cross'. That is, Bonhoeffer's theological ethics describe the way in which God makes it possible for human beings to act responsibly and obediently, without depriving them of their adulthood and human dignity. The extent to which Bonhoeffer's thinking is still useful today is something that only becomes clear as we read him and we will return explicitly to this question in the last chapter.

In the chapters that follow we will explore just what Dietrich Bonhoeffer meant by Christian ethics, or by what I have termed 'theological ethics'. For now I simply table the suggestion that this question underpins a good deal of his theological writing and his life, and it is to that life we can now turn.

Notes

1   For this and subsequent references to Auden, see *Auden*, Richard Davenport-Hines, Minerva, 1995.

2   Dictionary references are from the *Shorter Oxford English Dictionary*.

3   *Godless Morality: Keeping Religion out of Ethics*, Richard Holloway, Canongate, 1999.

4   *Karl Barth Letters 1961–1968*, T&T Clark, 1981, pp. 250–3.

5   Commenting on Barth's 1920s' lectures on ethics John Webster remarks that 'They deserve, for instance, to be more widely studied than Bonhoeffer's much more celebrated *Ethics*', *Barth's Moral Theology,* T&T Clark, Edinburgh, 1998, p. 61.

2

A life in dark times

'TO THOSE BORN LATER'

Truly, I live in dark times!
...
You who will emerge from the flood
In which we have gone under
Remember
When you speak of our failings
The dark time too
Which you have escaped.
For we went, changing countries oftener than our shoes
Through the wars of the classes, despairing
When there was injustice only, and no rebellion.

And yet we know:
Hatred, even of meanness
Contorts the features.
Anger, even against injustice
Makes the voice hoarse. Oh, we
Who wanted to prepare the ground for friendliness
Could not ourselves be friendly.

But you, when the time comes at last
And man is a helper to man

11

Think of us
With forbearance.[1]

Bertolt Brecht

Snapshot: July 1939

War was coming and everyone knew it. By the summer of 1939 preparations for defending the citizens of London were well under way. In September 1938 the Government had issued gas masks to every citizen in Britain. As the autumn wore on into the uncertain new year of 1939, bomb shelters were dug in the public parks, and in back gardens an Armada of Anderson shelters was fitted out and stocked up. In April 1939 a million extra burial forms were issued to London's local authorities in anticipation of bomb casualties; water pipes were enlarged so the fire services could douse the flames.[2] Few Britons faced the prospect of a new war with the same jingoism with which they had greeted the onset of the Great War twenty-five years earlier. Then, they had lost their men by the million but the sound of the guns had only rarely been audible in London. In the new war Britain's cities would be on the front line. In July 1939 the flotsam and jetsam of Europe's storms lapped against the steps of the British Museum where the poet Louis MacNeice perceived:

Between the enormous fluted Ionic columns
There seeps from heavily jowled or hawk-like foreign faces
The guttural sorrow of the refugees.[3]

At the same moment in Germany, the diarist Viktor Klemperer was fussing and fretting himself ready for the coming cataclysm. Of Jewish origin and a Great War veteran, Klemperer had more reason than most to hope war could be avoided. His diary reflects the tension in the city of Dresden and in Germany in which the atmosphere of expectancy was polluted by the still more sinister odour of fear. Klemperer's grocer expects Poland to be swallowed up by Germany as bloodlessly as Czechoslovakia; a friend thinks war will come by August; and a tram driver reports that a man with a Party badge suggested he change the English names of his children to German ones.[4]

Also in July 1939, in the London boarding house garden of a refugee family, Dietrich Bonhoeffer was photographed relaxing in a deck chair. The family of Gerhard Leibholz had arrived in London nine months earlier. Gerhard's wife Sabine was Bonhoeffer's twin and he felt as close to her as to anyone. In 1933 Bonhoeffer had obeyed his superior's instruction and refused Gerhard's request to conduct the funeral of his Jewish father (Bonhoeffer regretted his decision so bitterly that he later wrote a poignant apology to his brother-in-law[5]). Bonhoeffer had helped the family get out of Germany. In advance of their arrival in London he had written to influential British friends commending Gerhard's legal and political expertise. Now, travelling from New York to Germany, Bonhoeffer broke his journey to find out how the Leibholzes were settling in. His passport was due to expire in March 1940 and it was unlikely he would be granted another. Besides, the dogs of war were already growling and travel between Germany and Britain would soon be impossible. It is hardly surprising that a camera appeared and several pictures were taken.

In the photographs Bonhoeffer appears surprisingly at ease. A few days before he had taken the most difficult and significant decision of his life: to renounce personal security by returning from America to Germany in advance of war in order to participate in the anti-Nazi resistance. He was an intelligent man and his family and friends were well placed: he had the information to calculate the risk his return involved. The pictures show him listening earnestly, or smiling and talking. He is urbane and confident. Even in the summer sun he wears a tailored suit and matching tie. When these photographs were taken Bonhoeffer was 33 but looked middle-aged.

The letters Bonhoeffer sent to friends and family during his brief visit to London betray no sense of the turning point he had just passed.[6] He makes practical arrangements with his parents. In good English he writes to George Bell, Bishop of Chichester, explaining that the post of 'refugee Pastor' which he had been offered ought to go to one of his 'non-Aryan brethren who are much more entitled to such a post'. He asks Bell if anything can be done to support Gerhard Leibholz's application for a modest Church grant. At the end of the ten days Bonhoeffer left London as planned. He never saw his sister again.

Memory and history

'[A]fter great distance of time', wrote Thomas Hobbes, 'our imagination of the Past is weak ... so that *Imagination* and *Memory*, are but one thing.' There are too many ways in which memory and imagination get muddled for history to be a confident discipline, and this is nowhere truer than in the recent history of Germany. Hindsight embroiders facts and fogs truth: only by these means could one Nazi commander whose unit shot 15,000 people say at his trial that he was always 'inwardly opposed' to what he was doing.[7] History looks from the present into the past, but life is lived from the present towards the future. History can never report events just as they happened; we cannot, for example, look backwards into German history and forget the horror that resulted from Hitler's coming to power, or tell the life of Bonhoeffer and forget he was murdered. This incapacity to see things from the 'hindsightless' perspective of those who lived through the events we recall can lead us to attribute meaning to things that were not there at the time – poignantly noting for example that Bonhoeffer's meeting with his sister in 1939 was his last when neither of them could know it would be so. History-telling can also have a tendency to flatten out the complex ambiguities of events as they are lived to fit them into the historian's packaging; grey shades can be erased and a monochrome landscape remain peopled only by villains or saints. It is only with the benefit of an airbrushed memory that anything in twentieth-century German history looks this clear. The German people failed; the conspiracy against Hitler failed; the churches failed: Bonhoeffer shared in their failure. It is urgent that this awful history is remembered, but it will be better if our remembrance is graced by forbearance towards those who could not know the outcomes of their actions and inactions.

Most biographical accounts of Bonhoeffer collapse Germany's history, and that of the conspiracy and the church, into the story of Bonhoeffer's life. It is understandable that this should be the case. Yet while Bonhoeffer is naturally the central character in his own life-story, he was not central to these far broader contexts. Recounting the histories of Germany, the conspiracy and the church struggle from Bonhoeffer's perspective can illuminate them, but it can sometimes result in inflating his role. Within this chapter, therefore, I will try to embed Bonhoeffer's life within these broader contexts.

Germany: Empire, Republic and Reich

Dietrich Bonhoeffer's life spanned three eras in German history and two grim wars. The world into which he was born was very different from the one in which he died. On 4 February 1906 when Dietrich and his twin were delivered, Europe was a continent in which society was highly ordered, in which people knew their place, in which members of the upper classes found it instinctively difficult to be 'familiar' with the lower classes. Europe was at the end of an era of hierarchy: on the eve of the First World War there were just three Republics in Europe; by 1918 there would be thirteen. Few European societies were more formal than Germany under the Emperor Wilhelm II. Germany before the war was a patchwork quilt of former states each with its own culture, institutions and polity, gathered loosely into the Empire. But beneath this brittle exterior unity, tectonic plates of social and political life were shifting. Germany was undergoing a population explosion far in excess of neighbouring countries. In 1871 the German population was 41 million; in 1914 it was 67.7 million (to which the Bonhoeffer family's eight children made a handsome contribution). In the same period Germany experienced rapid industrial expansion; output increased fivefold while Britain's merely doubled. Cities and towns grew rapidly to accommodate these changes,[8] disrupting the comparatively stable social relations of the past and storing up industrial conflict and urban poverty for the future.

In 1906 Dietrich's father, Karl Bonhoeffer, was Professor of Psychiatry in Breslau (now Wrocław in Poland). In 1912 he moved to the prestigious Chair of Psychiatry and Neurology at Berlin University, where he consolidated his international reputation as a bulwark against new ideas in psychiatry flowing from Sigmund Freud and Carl Gustav Jung. This position, and the foreign currency that came from his publications, would insulate the Bonhoeffer family from some of the turmoil that was to come. Dietrich's mother Paula (née von Hase) came from a landowning family. Her father served for two years as the Emperor Wilhelm II's court preacher and became a Professor of Theology. In spite of this ecclesiastical heritage, like most Berliners, the Bonhoeffer family sat light to church membership. On the face of it Berlin, the Bonhoeffer family home and the German capital, was still a largely Protestant city. Even in 1933 over 70 per cent of the total population of 4.2 million designated themselves members of the provincial Evangelical (i.e. Protestant) Church.[9] Yet a large majority of them had lost any functioning connection with church life; estimates suggest that only 250,000–300,000 regularly participated in a worshipping congregation. When the Bonhoeffers required the services of the Church a relative came to the house to do the job. The family said evening prayers, sent their children to confirmation classes, and read the Bible; but a spirit of rational empiricism and liberalism most strongly characterized family life. Chatter and sentimentality were discouraged. Dietrich's brothers prepared for careers in science and law; his sisters married similarly solid professionals. So when Dietrich as a boy announced his decision to become a theologian his brothers discouraged him by pointing out how boring and petty church life was. Dietrich replied that he would reform it. Much later, in prison, Dietrich attempted to write a play in which one of his characters was strikingly like himself and to whom a remark is addressed that sums up the significance of the values and traditions that shaped him:

> People like you have a foundation, you have ground under your feet, you have a place in the world. There are things you take for granted, that you stand up for, and for which you are willing to put your head on the line, because you know your roots go so deep that they'll sprout new growth again. (*DBW 7*, 68)

This same seriousness was maintained when war was declared in 1914: when one of Bonhoeffer's sisters ran into the house shouting delightedly 'There's a war', she had her face slapped for being frivolous about events of such deadly seriousness.

In 1917 Bonhoeffer's two eldest brothers were called up; the next oldest followed a year later. In 1918 Dietrich's brother Walter was fatally wounded; the impact of his death on Bonhoeffer's family, most visibly his mother, was profound. Dietrich inherited his brother's Bible and used it for the rest of his life. In 1930/31 he wrote that 'I myself was in these years a schoolboy and I can assure you that not only had I in those days to learn what hunger means. I should wish that you would have to eat this food for only one day that we had for three or four years and I think you would get a glimpse of the privations which Germany had to endure [text amended]'.[10] Greater still was the war's impact on those returning from the front. One of those returning, Corporal Adolf Hitler, believed that the soldiers at the front had not lost the war at all. The war he believed, had been lost at home, where profiteering, poor morale and discipline, and above all the malign influence of Jews and Marxists had led to surrender when victory was still within reach. He was far from the only demobilized soldier to subscribe to this 'stab in the back' theory. Others simply felt destroyed spiritually and physically by what they had experienced: in Erich Maria Remarque's novel *All Quiet on the Western Front*, the protagonist, wounded and grieving the loss of friends, reflects on the future: 'I am young, I am twenty years old; yet I know nothing of life but despair, death, fear, and fatuous superficiality cast over an abyss of sorrow ... Our knowledge of life is limited to death. What will happen afterwards? And what shall come out of us?'

The period following the end of hostilities was marked in Germany by chaos, violence and bitterness. The Emperor fled and a Republic was declared. Dishevelled units of the collapsing army returned to Germany still carrying their rifles. Some formed bodies intent on armed insurrection; others formed 'Freikorps', armed volunteers loosely under the control of the army, to suppress them. A Soviet Republic was declared in Bavaria and viciously crushed. When Weimar was chosen as the town in which to inaugurate the new Republican constitution in 1919 it was not in tribute to the high culture of Goethe and Herder that had once flourished there, but because it was small enough to defend with two battalions of infantry. The Weimar constitution contained within it the seeds of its own destruction. Agreed in haste, it aimed to please everyone. Power on the one hand was too widely dispersed as Weimar Germany's electoral system necessitated weak government by coalition. On the other hand the President had too much power; he was both Commander in Chief of the Army and authorized to dissolve parliament. It is striking that the Nazis never needed to abolish the Weimar Constitution. But the bitterness of this time stemmed above all from Germany's reaction to the terms of the Versailles Treaty that ended the war. Germany ceded large areas of land to the victorious allies in the East and in the West. Germany was to pay crippling reparations to the victors over 42 years. A 'war guilt' clause fastened the blame for the war on Germany and Austria. Even in 1930/31 Bonhoeffer could describe this as 'the wound which still is open and bleeds in Germany'.[11] In March 1920 'Freikorps' units marched on Berlin and the army refused government orders to meet them. A General Strike restored order but an impression remained of the new democratic political system's incapacity to rule effectively. Political chaos gave way to economic chaos. As the revenue from tax was insufficient to pay the police, the army and the reparations bill, the government resorted to printing money and inflation galloped. In October 1923 Dietrich Bonhoeffer wrote to his parents telling them that each meal now cost 1 billion marks. By November 1923 the exchange rate was 4000 billion marks for one US dollar and the cash economy was replaced by an economy based on barter in which two eggs bought a theatre ticket and a pair of boots cost a pound of butter.

The student prince

In 1923 Dietrich began his theological studies, first in Tübingen and then in Berlin. The discipline of theology was undergoing a crisis of its own arising from war and political bedlam. In 1919, a Swiss Pastor, Karl Barth, published a commentary on Paul's letter to the Romans and in the same year he gave a lecture at Tambach in Germany on 'The Christian's Place in Society'. These two events marked the beginning of a new theological movement that would dominate western theology in the twentieth century. Barth demanded a revolution turning the attention of theology from human beings towards God in Christ. Barth had been shocked by the way that leading German academic theologians had supported the war. He was convinced that the Bible was not, as it was commonly regarded within the prevailing traditions of cultural Protestantism and liberal scholarship, merely a religious history or a book of Churchly doctrine, but a witness to the Bible writers' encounter with a living God. The theology faculty in Berlin was a bastion of just the kind of 'liberal' theology that Barth was challenging. Friedrich Schleiermacher, regarded as a father of Protestant liberal theology, had founded the theology faculty in Berlin; Adolf von Harnack, in his seventies in 1923 and a historian in the liberal school with an international reputation, still gave occasional classes in which Dietrich was a favourite student.

Barth's theology of crisis was not the only revolutionary theological movement current in Germany. Karl Holl, another of Bonhoeffer's teachers, was spearheading a revival of study into the theology of the Reformer Martin Luther. The Evangelical Church in Berlin was a united church containing both Lutheran and Reformed theological traditions, but Dietrich, as we shall see in the next chapter, was far more influenced by Luther than by Calvin, or indeed any other theologian. Dietrich also learned social theory and sociology from Ernst Troeltsch and dogmatic theology from Reinhold Seeberg, with whom he came into conflict when, after 1925, Bonhoeffer's essays began to incorporate Barth's influence. The conflict Bonhoeffer faced in the Berlin faculty is illustrated in a winsome letter to him from von Harnack complaining of the 'contempt for scientific theology and the menace posed by unscientific theology', in Barthianism. In 1924 Bonhoeffer spent a term in Rome and was deeply impressed both by this first encounter with classical antiquity and with the Roman Catholic Church, in which he sensed a seriousness and universalism far removed from the caricatures of the Roman church served up in Protestant Berlin. A year later, aged nineteen, Bonhoeffer began work on his doctoral dissertation alongside his other studies. His Roman experiences influenced his choice of topic, a study of the Church. He achieved the licentiate degree, the Berlin equivalent of a Doctorate, in 1927 with his dissertation *Sanctorum Communio: A Theological Study of the Sociology of the Church*. The same year he began training for ordination within his regional church.

In the late 1920s and early 1930s Weimar Germany was, in George Orwell's phrase, 'a society in decay'. Politics still had a tendency to spill violently onto the streets. In the cafés, clubs and beer-cellars of Berlin a jazzy counter-culture developed that troubled instinctively conservative middle-class Protestant families like the Bonhoeffers. This was the Berlin described in Christopher Isherwood's book *Goodbye to Berlin* on which the musical *Cabaret* was based. Isherwood's characters populate a city where wealth and poverty live cheek by jowl in smoky nightclubs thriving on drink and prostitution. We should remember that the word 'kitsch' is German. Many Germans felt that the Weimar Republic was presiding over an unprecedented period of moral decline emblematized by growing numbers of women smoking in public, wearing their hair short and doubtless using contraceptives!

The party passed Bonhoeffer by. All indicators pointed towards an academic career for him, but Bonhoeffer felt at least as strongly drawn to the ministry of preaching and pastoral care. At the beginning of 1928 he took a post as assistant Minister of the German congregation in Barcelona. He took to congregational life and to Spain; he even relished bullfighting. But, though invited to remain, he returned to Berlin early in 1929. Partly to pursue his genuine theological interests, and partly to evade attendance at his regional church's preacher's seminary, he began work on his *Habilitation*, the post-doctoral degree that would qualify him as a university lecturer. Alongside his research and writing he took a job as a voluntary assistant lecturer in the Berlin faculty. He submitted his second dissertation, *Act and Being*, in 1930. Both this and *Sanctorum Communio* were subsequently published, though with a signal lack of success.

New York

In September Bonhoeffer travelled to the United States to take up a scholarship at Union Seminary in New York. At least as much as his previous years of study, life at Union shaped Bonhoeffer's outlook on life. In some of his papers and lectures, even taking into account that he is writing in a newly acquired language, Bonhoeffer seems over-earnest. America really was an alien land that took some getting used to: he apparently failed his driving test because he refused to pay the normal bribe to the examiner. The theological foundations and perspectives of American student peers were typically very different to his own rigorous Berlin education; he winced as fellow students laughed when Luther was quoted in lectures. But in the Frenchman, Jean Lasserre, Bonhoeffer first encountered a Christian pacifism that would constitute a prominent theme in his writings for the following decade. With Lasserre Bonhoeffer watched the film version of Remarque's *All Quiet on the Western Front*; the German and the Frenchman were united in disgust for the manner in which the American audience trivialized what was for them both a gut-wrenching story. Bonhoeffer preferred the 'Negro' churches of Harlem to the alternatives because he thought that the gospel was authentically preached in them; he participated in youth work in a Harlem church there with a fellow Union student, Frank Fisher. He was struck by the ways in which 'the social gospel' was taught and preached in the United States, particularly by his teacher at Union, Reinhold Niebuhr. But though he applauded the attempt to relate the gospel to social and political life – still very rare in Germany – his final judgement on American Christianity was that it amounted to 'Protestantism without Reformation'.

Work

Bonhoeffer's return to Germany in 1931 marked the beginning of his life as a teacher and a pastor. In the summer of 1931 he attended an Ecumenical conference in Cambridge. At first, his involvement in the nascent ecumenical movement was relatively insignificant, but it came to occupy a central part in his life with the onset of the church struggle. He was ordained in November – an event to which at the time he attached little significance – and assigned to a student chaplaincy at the technical college in Charlottenburg; it was not a ministry that proved fruitful. He was at the time, as Eberhard Bethge put it, a systematic theologian 'searching for the preacher' (*DB* 182). Bethge believes that Bonhoeffer underwent a transformation at this stage from being a theologian to being a Christian.[12] In a letter of 1936 Bonhoeffer described how, at this stage, 'something happened, something that has changed and transformed my life to the present day. For the first time I discovered the Bible ... I had often preached, I had seen a great deal of the church, spoken and preached about it – but I had not yet become a Christian' (*DB* 205).

Germany in 1932 was a country in economic and political chaos. The German economy had been hit badly by the sudden withdrawal of international capital following the Wall Street crash in October 1929. Between 1929 and 1932 industrial production in Germany fell by 42 per cent.[13] The German banks collapsed in 1931. As a symptom of economic uncertainty unemployment, at 1.3 million in 1929, rose to over 6 million by the beginning of 1933, and even this figure, one in three of the working population, is likely to be an underestimate of families affected.[14] The payment of unemployment benefits by those in work to those out of work could not be sustained, and failure to find a solution led in March 1930 to the abandonment of parliamentary government and to the direct appointment of a cabinet by the President. To some extent the chaos suited the old military, political and business élites as it fitted with their aim of bringing an end to Germany's payment of war reparations. But the inability of the centre parties and of the Social Democrats to address unemployment led to popular disillusionment with parliamentary democracy and a willingness to try extreme solutions. The Communist Party was the main political beneficiary, but the situation also made the Nazis more plausible. In the 1928 elections the NSDAP (the Nazi Party) achieved just 2.6 per cent of the vote, but in September 1930 they become the second largest party in the Reichstag with 107 deputies. In July 1932 the NSDAP gained 230 seats, though this was eroded in elections in November of the same year. Significantly as context for Bonhoeffer's lectures, the middle classes were just as disillusioned with politics as young working men and women: support for the NSDAP among university students was disproportionately high, and this was particularly true of theology students.[15] Indeed, at the root of Nazi success was its claim that while other parties represented interest groups – the Communists and Social Democrats for the workers; the Centre Party for Catholics; the Liberals for businessmen – their party was a party for all Germans. The failure to govern by Germany's traditional élites and the momentum of Nazi electoral successes persuaded President Hindenburg to appoint Hitler Chancellor on 30 January 1933. Thereafter, Hitler moved swiftly to consolidate his power. Using the Reichstag fire as a pretext – Bonhoeffer's father would later write the psychological report on the man accused of starting it

– Hitler declared a state of emergency, and on 23 March, after considerable intimidation, he passed the Enabling Laws allowing him to govern without recourse to parliamentary approval. A year later the first concentration camp opened at Dachau, providing the state with the option of detaining opponents without full process of the law. On 30 June, 'the night of the long knives', Hitler acted to remove any potential opposition within the Party and the country. When President Hindenberg died in the summer of 1934 it was an easy matter for Hitler to abolish the post and require the armed forces to swear allegiance to him instead. It had taken Hitler a couple of years to step from the political fringe to a position of unassailable and apparently permanent power.

These political events were taking place literally outside the door of Bonhoeffer's lecture theatre and exposed fundamental questions of political life: in a setting where democracy appeared to have failed where was political authority to derive from? What is the proper nature of power and what the nature of authority? Events also exposed theological questions concerning the role of the Church in politics. As a *privatdozent* (an authorized lecturer not on the Faculty payroll) Bonhoeffer had a free hand in choosing what he taught. His choices had to be registered, but he was not constrained overmuch by the oversight of his Faculty. In the summer of 1932 he lectured on 'The nature of the church' and led a seminar on the topic 'Is there a Christian ethic?' During the winter Bonhoeffer lectured on 'Recent Theology', and led a seminar on 'Dogmatics: Problems of a theological anthropology'. He also gave a series of lectures on Genesis 1–3. Bonhoeffer was pressed by students to publish the text of his lectures and did so under the title *Creation and Fall*. It is the only series of lectures Bonhoeffer gave in his two years as a lecturer in Berlin to survive in Bonhoeffer's own words; his other lectures, including his lectures in the summer semester of 1933 on *Christology*, survive only in notes taken by students.

Bonhoeffer's lectures on *Creation and Fall* effected a new theological engagement with politics. On 1 February 1933, two days after the Berlin crowds had enthusiastically acclaimed Hitler's appointment as Reich Chancellor, Bonhoeffer gave a radio broadcast on 'The Younger Generation's Altered View of the Concept of the *Führer*', a topic he had planned before Hitler assumed power. The politically controversial nature of the address may be the reason it was cut off before Bonhoeffer had finished speaking. It was not the loss of democracy that troubled Bonhoeffer in the collapse of the Weimar constitution, but the loss of the law, the loss of the limits that constrain office holders in the exercise of their authority. Bonhoeffer's anxiety was that the Führer – leader – was becoming a verführer – a misleader – for the younger generation. Bonhoeffer also recognized that anti-Semitism was central to Nazi ideology, and this too disturbed him. In Germany, clergy were regarded in a sense as civil servants. When the Nazis introduced legislation to ban Jews, and those of Jewish origin, from holding an appointment as a civil servant they also attempted to impose this 'Aryan Paragraph' on the Church. For Bonhoeffer, erecting a racial criterion for participation in the Church created a *'status confessionis,'* that is it confronted the Church with a theological heresy so significant that Christians could not accept it without denying their confession that Jesus Christ is Lord. A Church that accepted such a policy removed itself from God's blessing.[16] His views set him on a collision course with the Nazi state.

The Church struggle

At this stage in Bonhoeffer's life the 'Church struggle' as it has become known, began increasingly to absorb his energies. The struggle within the German Protestant churches, and between the churches and the Nazi State, was involved, complex, and is too infrequently explained to English speakers new to Bonhoeffer's life. When Hitler was appointed Reich Chancellor in 1933 there were 28 regional Evangelical (i.e. Protestant) Churches in Germany that before German unification had each been national Churches. Some were purely Lutheran in church tradition, others Reformed; some, like Bonhoeffer's regional Church in Prussia, united Lutheran and Reformed traditions. In some regions, particularly in southern Germany, Catholics were in the majority, in others, particularly in the north, Protestants were in a majority. Adolf Hitler lacked patience with German Protestantism and understood it even less. But Hitler, by birth an Austrian Catholic, understood from Fascists in Italy, to whom he initially looked up, the importance of 'neutering' Catholic opposition. This was particularly significant in Germany where the lay Catholic Centre Party provided a significant political and electoral obstacle to Nazi ambitions. In the 1920 programme of the Nazi party, declared unalterable by Hitler in 1926, Article 24 had guaranteed 'freedom for all religious confessions in the state' and gone even further in stating that the 'Party as such stands for a positive Christianity, without binding itself denominationally to a particular confession'. This note of 'positive Christianity' contrasted with the overt hostility of the Communists and the ambivalence of the Social Democrats towards Christian religion.

In 1933 the Nazis negotiated a Reich Concordat with the Vatican over the heads of the German Catholic Bishops, who had previously banned Catholics from Nazi Party membership. The Catholic Centre Party was disbanded as a condition of the agreement. The Vatican Secretary of State, Eugenio Pacelli, who became Pope Pius XII in 1939, led the Vatican negotiations. By 1933 the Nazi policy of 'gleichschaltung' – coordination – was in full swing: all organizations from sports clubs to boy scout troops were coming under the National Socialist movement either voluntarily or by force. Predictably Hitler wanted the regional Protestant Churches also to fall in line, and unification of the regional Churches under one Reich Bishop was the obvious way to begin this process. The Free Churches (i.e. Protestant churches who were not historically national churches), who made up a relatively minor proportion of Christians in Germany, maintained their nominal independence by agreeing to all the state's demands. But opinion within the regional Churches was mixed. At one end of the spectrum of opinion were those like Bonhoeffer who opposed state interference in church life as a matter of theological principle (not all of these were anti-Nazi); at the opposite end of the spectrum others felt that the national reform the Nazis were leading presaged a necessary reform of the Church and therefore supported Nazi plans. The struggle focused on elections for the office of Reich Bishop and Church Parties were formed as vehicles for these poles of opinion.

The pro-Nazi Church Party called themselves the *Deutsche Christen* – German Christians (sometimes abbreviated as DC). A 1933 manifesto for Church elections embodies their self-perception:

> The German Christians are Jesus Christ's S.A. [i.e. *Sturmabteilung* – Brownshirts] ... They march with this watchword: Germany, through Christ, a people of God ... Even as the National-Socialistic movement for freedom is the plant-cell of a new nation and marches towards the goal 'There must become one German nation', so the German Christians are called to be the plant-cell of the new German Evangelical Church, and they march towards the goal 'There must become one church'.[17]

The regional Churches were very largely led by men in their sixties and seventies, while German Christian candidates for high ecclesiastical office were often much younger, contributing to the impression that the German Christians were vigorous and revolutionary. The 'opposition' was slower to materialize. A Young Reformers Movement, which Bonhoeffer signed up to, had emerged early on but petered out. In September 1933 a Pastors' Emergency League was formed led by the Dahlem Pastor Martin Niemöller. Niemöller had been a U-boat commander in the first war, was highly decorated, and had at first supported the Nazis: his decision now to lead the church opposition contributed to its credibility. Bonhoeffer was very junior by comparison, but was nonetheless one of the nucleus of Berlin clergy around whom the Emergency league coalesced. They were united in opposition but split by competing ideas and motivation.

Two candidates emerged from the two church groups for the post of Reich Bishop. Ludwig Müller was a military chaplain who had inveigled himself into an appointment as Hitler's personal representative in Protestant Church affairs. The Führer's nod was as good as a wink for the German Christians and Müller, who had few personal qualities otherwise to recommend him, soon became their candidate. To oppose him the Emergency League persuaded Friedrich von Bodelschwingh, director of a community for the disabled in Bethel, and a man of irreproachable personal integrity. Representatives of regional churches and church bodies in a complex Electoral College cast votes and somewhat to everyone's surprise Bodelschwingh was overwhelmingly elected. This marked the high point of Protestant opposition to Hitler, whose wishes had been ignored. But the appearance of united opposition to Hitler's plans for the Protestant churches proved illusory. The German Christians disputed Bodelschwingh's election on technical grounds and within days his authority was being undermined. Bodelschwingh had no stomach for a fight characterized by shameful German Christian animus towards him and he resigned. In the elections that followed Müller was elected Reich Bishop.

It is easy to get the impression from all this, and from Bonhoeffer's letters and papers from this period, that the 'German Church Struggle' involved all Protestant Christians in a bitter, time-consuming controversy. To be sure, by January 1934 the Pastors' Emergency League had 7000 members nationally, a significant proportion of the total number of ordained Protestant clergy. The Church historian Manfred Gailus gives a detailed picture of the extent of the Church opposition in Bonhoeffer's regional Church in Berlin:

[O]f 565 pastors with a congregation in Berlin during the Nazi period, a church-political orientation could be determined for 509. Of these, 44 per cent belonged to the DC camp either throughout or for part of the period. A good 36 per cent belonged to the opposite BK [i.e. Confessing Church] camp.[18]

The remainder oscillated between the two sides or deliberately kept out of 'church politics'. Yet while a high proportion of clergy were involved, a relatively small proportion of church members for whom an affiliation can be discerned took any part. At the height of the conflict, from 1936 to 1939, Confessing Church groups in Berlin's 147 parishes probably involved around 36,000 people (compared with 50,000 members aligned to the German Christians). At least three quarters of Confessing Church members in Berlin were women, though the twenty member Berlin leadership body had no women members. The whole church struggle was waged, at least in Berlin, by minorities amongst the church's members. Based on the church elections in the summer of 1933, the affiliation of 131 of Berlin's 147 parishes can be ascribed: 34 parishes were basically Nazified; 21 were prepared to conform to the German Christian plans; 68 were split between the two poles of the conflict and at most eight parishes were 'resistant', i.e. clearly aligned with the church opposition.[19]

Shortly after the apparent success of the German Christians in the election of Ludwig Müller they scored a damaging own goal. A keynote address on 13 November 1933 at a German Christian rally held in the Berlin Sports Palace called for the Old Testament to be scrapped, for the 'scapegoat and inferiority theology of the rabbi Paul' to be excised from the Church, and allegiance declared to Jesus Christ as a heroic Aryan type. Widespread resignations from the movement followed. In spite of this setback, German Christians in many regional churches held key appointments or were in majorities on decision-making bodies. To focus opposition into a 'Confessing Church' Bonhoeffer was asked, with a colleague, to draft a confession of faith, a statement that might summarize and express the heart of theological opposition. But when Bonhoeffer presented the document to the representatives who had commissioned it they insisted on redrafting the more 'controversial' sections on the Old Testament and the Jews with the result that, from Bonhoeffer's perspective, the statement was eviscerated. He refused to sign, and his disillusionment was a contributory factor behind his decision to take up the Parish minister's job in London in October 1933. A year later Karl Barth had greater success with drafting a

26

statement for a Confessing Church Synod held at Barmen. The Barmen Declaration finally gave the disparate Confessing groups a theological foundation with Christ as its cornerstone. It was followed by a second synod at Dahlem, which drew out some of the practical and legal consequences. In the nascent international ecumenical movement Bonhoeffer, a 'youth delegate', consistently urged Church leaders to recognize the Confessing Church in Germany as the *only* Protestant Church. He was to be disappointed: the ecumenical movement attempted to appear impartial and invited representatives of both 'churches' to meetings, as though the Confessing Church were a new breakaway denomination. To Bonhoeffer this badly missed the theological point, which was that the Confessing Church had not 'left' the German national Church; it *was* the national Church, and the German Christians had set themselves outside the Church and beyond the salvation of Christ.

Though during Bonhoeffer's two years as a lecturer in Berlin he had become increasingly involved both in the ecumenical movement and in opposition to state interference in church life, he had not lost his thirst for international travel or his sense of calling to a ministry of preaching and pastoral care. He became interested in the non-violent political action advocated by Gandhi and through George Bell, Bishop of Chichester, whom Bonhoeffer had met in the context of the ecumenical movement, he explored the possibility of living at Gandhi's Ashram – an unfulfilled ambition he did not give up until 1935. In October 1933 he took a job as Pastor to two German-speaking congregations in London, living in Forest Gate in south London. Bonhoeffer thrived on local church life but the Confessing Church needed him at home and he returned in April 1935.

Seminary Director

Preacher's seminaries were a recent innovation in Germany. Pastors undertook theological studies in a university setting and, in the past, were ordained with little training in preaching and pastoral care. The seminary Bonhoeffer was appointed to direct was one of five established in 1934 and 1935 by his regional Church, the Old Prussian Council of Brethren, now severely disrupted by the Church struggle. Bonhoeffer held this post until his death, though he was later technically 'on leave'. The seminary was an uncertain venture: students relied on gifts to pay their expenses and there was no certainty that 'graduates' could be placed in pastorates. The seminary met first in Zingst and later in Finkenwalde near Stettin (now Szczecin in

Poland). Bonhoeffer's attempts to integrate academic theology with Christian community living and practical preparation for ministry seemed strange, at first, to students used to academic study alone. A good sense of life in the seminary can be gleaned from the two books Bonhoeffer wrote at Finkenwalde: *Discipleship* (1937) and *Life Together* (1939), both discussed in Chapter 6. Bonhoeffer's lectures on 'discipleship' were also delivered at the Faculty in Berlin; they were the last lectures Bonhoeffer gave there before his licence to teach in the university was withdrawn in August 1936.

Alongside the seminary Bonhoeffer established a 'House of Brethren', in which half a dozen course 'graduates' lived who each held local church posts. The House of Brethren was intended to model a community of proclamation and communal living and to offer a retreat centre for working pastors in the Confessing Church. But very soon a noose began to tighten around the life of the seminary and the House of Brethren. Five groups of students undertook their course at the seminary before the Gestapo closed the seminary in September 1937. The House of Brethren was disbanded a short while after. In place of the seminary Bonhoeffer established a number of 'collective pastorates' in which ministerial candidates could be placed in 'apprenticeships' with sympathetic pastors, but still be guided by him in their training. Bonhoeffer diligently maintained links with former students and their families; many had run into difficulties with the Police. This was a frustrating time for Bonhoeffer, who no longer had a settled base from which to work. In January 1938 he was questioned by the Gestapo following a church meeting in Berlin, put on a train out of the city, and prohibited from returning. Bonhoeffer found ways around the ban but he had to be cautious.

In 1938 the dark shadow of Nazi ambitions spread over Germany and over Europe. In March German troops marched into Austria, whose Government instructed the Austrian Army to offer no resistance. Austrians greeted the *Anschluss* with widespread enthusiasm.[20] Throughout the year Hitler skilfully manipulated the European powers. Possibly blinded to the true nature of Nazi objectives, the British Prime Minister Neville Chamberlain agreed Hitler's aims at a conference in Munich, claiming the agreement guaranteed 'peace in our time'. Under this agreement Germany annexed the Sudetenland across its south-eastern border ostensibly to protect the interests of the German speakers there; by the following year Bohemia, Moravia and Slovakia had become German protectorates. Within Germany there was an increase in anti-Semitic actions climaxing on 9 November 1938 with *'Kristallnacht'*, the night of broken glass when Nazi activists and German sympathizers burned Synagogues, looted Jewish-owned shops and businesses, and enacted violence on Jews. In his Bible Bonhoeffer wrote the date of *Kristallnacht* beside Psalm 74:8: 'they burned all the meeting places of God in the land'. Bonhoeffer was one of a very few within the Confessing Church who considered solidarity with the Jews, and not just Jews who had converted to Christianity, a matter on which the Church must stake its life. The Church in Germany had proved incapable of effective resistance to the Nazis; he would have to look elsewhere now for a means by which to act. A split had become apparent in the Confessing Church between regional Lutheran churches, that were more or less free of German Christians and of state interference, and Confessing Christians in divided regional Churches such as Prussia. The split contributed, in the wake of a solidification of Nazi social control, to the Confessing Church's growing tendency to turn in on itself, as if it was enough to preserve its own institutional interests while leaving the state a free hand in all other matters, such as persecution of the Jews. This tendency was even more pronounced following the controversial trial of Martin Niemöller in March 1938. When he was effectively acquitted of alleged subversive activities, Hitler intervened to intern Niemöller as a personal prisoner of the Führer. He remained in a concentration camp until the end of war.

Double agent

Thus disillusioned, in 1938 Bonhoeffer made first contact with a hub of anti-Nazi sentiment in the *Abwehr*, the German military intelligence agency, where his brother-in-law, Hans von Dohnanyi was a senior legal advisor. He sensed that if he stayed in Germany he would feel it necessary to be drawn into the conspiracy against Hitler: it was a far from natural course of action for a pastor and a theologian who had advanced Christian pacifism. He made a will. In March and April 1939 Bonhoeffer travelled to England to nurture his ecumenical contacts; he took the opportunity to put out feelers towards America. In May, as he had been dreading, his call-up for military service reached him. Made aware of his dilemmas American friends contrived an invitation for him to travel to the United States. A number of possible options were set in motion including lecturing, or a job as pastor to German refugees. Again travelling via England he reached New York in June. But his uneasiness with this route to the future had deepened. On 22 June Bonhoeffer wrote in his diary: 'To be here during a catastrophe is simply unthinkable, unless things are so ordained. But to be guilty of it myself, and to have to reproach myself that I left unnecessarily, is certainly devastating.' On 28 June he added: 'I cannot imagine that it is God's will for me to remain here without anything particular to do in case of war. I must travel at the first possible opportunity' (*DB* 656). He came to a decision: in July he wrote to his sponsor Reinhold Niebuhr:

> I have made a mistake in coming to America. I must live through this difficult period in our national history with the Christian people of Germany. I will have no right to participate in the reconstruction of Christian life in Germany after the war if I do not share in the trials of this time with my people ... Christians in Germany will face the terrible alternative of either willing the defeat of their nation in order that Christian civilization may survive, or willing the victory of their nation and thereby destroying our civilization. I know which of these alternatives I must choose; but I cannot make that choice in security. (*DB* 655)

No amount of urging from Reinhold Niebuhr and Paul Lehmann could change his mind. Lehmann accompanied him on board the ship to Britain still trying to keep Bonhoeffer back. He left New York on 7 July; on the 27th he was home in Berlin. The German invasion of Poland began on 1 September and Europe was again at war.

The initial progress of the German army was astonishing. Poland fell in under three weeks and was partitioned with the collusion of the Soviet Union. By May 1940 Norway, Holland and Belgium were under German occupation. Germany had spent most of the First World War bogged down in Belgian and French mud; the surrender of France in the summer of 1940 seemed to right all the wrongs of the conflict a generation earlier. When news of the French surrender was announced over the radio Bonhoeffer and Eberhard Bethge were in a café in Memel. The crowd was jubilant and to Bethge's surprise Bonhoeffer joined them in giving the Hitler salute: 'we shall have to run risks for very different things now, but not for that salute' he explained. History was being made; people were dying and Bonhoeffer was giving Bible studies to German villagers: he needed to act and doors were closing all around. In 1940 the Gestapo closed down the Collective Pastorates and Bonhoeffer was out of a job. In March 1941 he was forbidden to publish because of his 'subversive activities'. In order to avoid conscription and to situate himself within the anti-Nazi conspiracy, Bonhoeffer became a civilian member of the German Military Intelligence, who justified his role on the basis that his international ecumenical contacts yielded useful information. It was a strange moment to join the conspiracy. Before the war many German generals had treated Hitler's predictions of rapid success with scepticism: with Corporal Hitler proved right so spectacularly the possibility of a military coup for the moment passed. Removing Hitler would be a long game.

Upon the outbreak of war a kind of rapprochement took place between the churches and the Nazi state, as many who had previously doubted the regime patriotically put themselves behind the war effort. For their part, the Nazis were content to bide their time in relation to Christianity. Josef Goebbels, Hitler's 'Minister of Public Enlightenment and Propaganda' recorded in a diary entry in 1939 the true nature of Nazi policy towards the churches in wartime:

> The best way to deal with the churches is to claim to be a positive Christian ... the technique must be to hold back for the present and coolly strangle any attempts at impudence or interference in the affairs of the state ... He [Hitler] views Christianity as a symptom of decay. Rightly so. It is a branch of the Jewish race.

The policy, in other words, was to permit a certain freedom to the churches during wartime with the intention of crushing them when victory was complete. Yet the war also revealed the criminal character of the Nazis more clearly, and this resulted in the one confrontation of church and state that had genuinely successful results. This was when, after war began, a euthanasia programme was initiated to kill off people considered an unnecessary drain on the nation's resources in war: these included the mentally disabled, the severely mentally ill, those with extreme dementia or epilepsy, as well as some with physical disability. The method was to order a transfer of a patient or group of patients to another unnamed institution. Soon after a note would inform relatives that the patient had died. Church-based institutions carried out a good deal of care and treatment for people in these 'categories', and it was apparent, even to the most credulous, that a large number of people were being murdered. Opposition to the programme had evidence that was difficult to refute; confronted in this way the state called off the programme at the end of 1941, shortly before the Wannsee

Conference, which initiated the 'Final Solution' of the Jewish 'problem'.

Bonhoeffer's life as an agent of the Military Intelligence left him plenty of time to think, and the period from mid-1940 to his arrest in 1943 was theologically among the most fruitful of his life. Bonhoeffer turned his attention once more to ethics, which enabled him to integrate theology with the events in which he was engaged; the results, fragmentary and brilliant, are discussed in Chapter 7. His strengthening theological hold on daily life corresponded with a momentous personal development when in January 1943 Bonhoeffer became engaged, secretly at first because she was only eighteen years old, to Maria von Wedemeyer. Maria's grandmother was one of Bonhoeffer's most ardent supporters during his Directorship of the seminary and the pastorates; her father and brother were army officers killed in the war. It was an unusual alliance; intense, life-giving and strained by the war and the conspiracy, his involvement in which Bonhoeffer did not fully disclose.[21] On behalf of Military Intelligence Bonhoeffer travelled three times to Switzerland, twice to Sweden, and once to Norway during 1941 and 1942. But in spite of all the care and caution taken by the conspirators within Military Intelligence, tracks had been left. In 1942 the Gestapo began investigating *Abwehr* activities. Von Dohnanyi received a warning that his telephone and post were under surveillance; a routine request for a visa for Dietrich went unanswered. On 5 April 1943 Bonhoeffer, who was working on his ethics at his parents' house in Berlin, telephoned his sister Christine von Dohnanyi and a stranger answered. Dietrich knew at once that the man was a Gestapo officer. He cleared his desk and went next door to his sister Ursula's and ate a good meal. Shortly after his father came to tell him that 'there are two men wanting to speak to you upstairs in your room'.

Imprisonment

Tegel was a military interrogation prison and though a civilian, Bonhoeffer was held there as a member of the *Abwehr*. Bonhoeffer's first days there were grim. Mentally he had prepared himself for this moment, but his isolation and the conditions penetrated his soul. He was unaccustomed to incivility and brutality. At this early stage his investigators did not suspect his involvement in a plot to assassinate the Führer. When he was finally charged, it was with 'subversion of the armed forces' because he had 'evaded' conscription and helped at least one other to do so. The *Abwehr* was also under investigation for its role in an operation, in which Bonhoeffer was personally involved, smuggling Jews to Switzerland. Bonhoeffer's relative Lieutenant General Paul von Hase – who would later pay with his life for his own involvement in the resistance – was military governor of Berlin and visited him in the prison with several bottles of wine and pointedly talked and laughed with his nephew. After the visit Bonhoeffer was treated with more respect. As the months of Bonhoeffer's imprisonment wore on he adapted to the routine. His family brought him food, clothes, books and tobacco. He exercised, read extensively and tried his hand at writing poetry, a play and a novel. A sympathetic guard smuggled letters in and out of his cell; by this avenue we have the correspondence published after the war as Bonhoeffer's *Letters and Papers from Prison*. In prison Bonhoeffer was as much in danger from allied bombing as from the investigation; he lost patience with others' fear – and he lost a friend to a direct hit.

In July 1944 an assassination attempt was made on Hitler's life. Bonhoeffer knew it was coming and his smuggled letters reflect both his patience and impatience to know the outcome. In October 1944 evidence came to light linking him with the attempted assassination. He was transferred to the Gestapo prison in Prinz Albrecht Strasse and his links with family and friends were abruptly ended. In February 1945 Bonhoeffer was moved again, this time to the Buchenwald concentration camp, then to Regensburg and Schönberg. He developed relationships with those who shared his confinement and journeys. One, British officer Payne Best, later recalled that Bonhoeffer never complained but was, rather, 'quite calm and normal; seemingly perfectly at his ease ... his soul really shone in the dark desperation of our prison'. With a Soviet prisoner, Kokorin – a nephew of Molotov – Bonhoeffer learned Russian in exchange for lessons in the rudiments of Christian theology. On the Sunday after Easter a group of fellow prisoners asked Bonhoeffer to conduct a service for them. At first he was reluctant in deference to the Catholics and Atheists among the group, but when Kokorin approved, he agreed. He explained the texts for the day 'With his wounds we are healed' (Isaiah 53:5) and 'Blessed be the God and Father of our Lord Jesus Christ! By his great mercy we have been born anew to a living hope through the resurrection of Jesus Christ from the dead' (1 Peter 1:3). When news spread to other groups that he had led worship, they wanted him to repeat it for them, but there was no time. A call came for 'Prisoner Bonhoeffer'. He knew what it meant and wrote his name and address in a book he had with him as evidence of his final movements for his family. He asked Payne Best to pass a message to George Bell: 'this is the end – for me the beginning of life'.

Bonhoeffer was transferred to Flossenbürg concentration camp. A personal order from Hitler had condemned him a few days earlier and had now caught up with him. During the night Bonhoeffer and others from the *Abwehr* including Admiral Canaris and Brigadier General Oster were summarily tried. At dawn they were ordered to undress. The SS camp doctor – present to certify death – later reported that before he complied Bonhoeffer knelt and prayed. At the gallows he again prayed before composedly climbing the steps. The bodies and possessions of those executed were burned. His brother-in-law Hans von Dohnanyi was killed the same day at Sachsenhausen; on 23 April his brother Klaus and brother-in-law Rüdiger Schleicher were executed. On 30 April Adolf Hitler did what the conspirators had failed to do and ended his own life.

The conspiracy to assassinate Hitler

In writing of the German opposition to Adolf Hitler, as Alan Bullock has rightly noted, there is a danger 'of giving altogether too sharp a picture of what was essentially a number of small, loosely connected groups, fluctuating in membership, with no common organization and no common purpose other than their hostility to the existing régime'.[22] The circumstances of conspiracy made it difficult for individuals and groups to coordinate their actions and contributed to the insular and individualistic character of the resistance. But even taking into account evident differences of political opinion among the conspirators it is fair to say, as Mary Fulbrook does, that 'most of them were essentially anti-democratic in outlook. They wanted an authoritarian government run by elites, and not a return to the sort of constitution embodied in the Weimar Republic; they disliked the idea of mass participation in government, and had little conception of the need for popular legitimation of a new government.'[23]

Bonhoeffer's own role was relatively minor compared to that of Hans von Dohnanyi, his brother-in-law. Yet he knew a great many details of the conspiracy, more than enough fatally to incriminate himself and many others. The demands of coordinating his evidence to the investigating magistrate with that of his colleagues in order to conceal the conspiracy while adequately defending himself against the lesser charges on which he was initially arrested were immense.

Before his arrest the *Abwehr* protected him from conscription. With his *Abwehr* passport he was able to travel to neutral and occupied countries, and through his ecumenical contacts encourage churchly resistance to Nazi policy. On one of these trips, Bonhoeffer travelled with Helmut Count von Moltke, the central figure in the 'Kreisau Circle', an 'adjacent' resistance group to that in the *Abwehr*. Von Moltke's motivation, like Bonhoeffer's, arose from deep Christian convictions, but von Moltke did not approve of assassination as a means to their common objectives. In May 1942 Bonhoeffer and his clerical colleague Hans Schönfeld, met Bishop George Bell in Stockholm and through him passed a message to the British Foreign Secretary, Anthony Eden, sounding him out on the Allied response to a potential coup. Eden replied to Bell's report on the meeting that he was 'satisfied that it was not in the national interest to provide an answer of any kind'. When Bell pressed the matter again Eden made a marginal note on his draft reply that 'I see no reason whatsoever to encourage this pestilent priest'.[24] It is difficult to see how the Allies could have reacted any differently and there is a jarring naivety in Bonhoeffer's hope that they might. But the circle of which Dietrich Bonhoeffer was a member came closest of all the resistance groups to succeeding. The bomb placed by von Stauffenberg beneath a table in the 'Wolf's Lair' at Rastenberg devastated the room; its force blew Hitler's clothes from him, but left him relatively unharmed. Even then, the coup might have won through, but matters slipped out of the conspirators' hands, and the Nazis were in full control by the following day.

Joachim Fest raises the question of what, had it succeeded, the bomb plot would have achieved, and draws the 'sobering' conclusion that 'nothing would have changed. The Allies would not have altered their aims, abandoning their demand for unconditional surrender, nor would they have modified the decision made later at Yalta to occupy and divide Germany'.[25] Yet, as Fest also notes, the stakes proved tragically high as a ceasefire in July 1944 had the potential to save a great many German lives – to say nothing of others' lives: from the outbreak of war up to July 1944 2.8 million German soldiers and civilians died, while from July 1944 until the end of the war in Europe 4.8 million were killed.[26] The day after the assassination attempt had failed Bonhoeffer's brother Klaus, Emmi his wife and her brother Justus Delbrück were clearing bomb wreckage from a friend's house when Emmi asked the men what lesson they drew from the failure of the plot. Delbrück's reply, as Fest observes, captures the pathos and paradox of the resistance: 'I think it was good that it happened, and good too, perhaps, that it did not succeed'.[27] Bonhoeffer's own assessment of the failure of the conspiracy and of the Church was harsher. But towards women and men of such courage, ultimately Brecht's request should surely be granted:

Remember
When you speak of our failings ...

Think of us
With forbearance.

Notes

1   'To Those Born Later', Bertolt Brecht, tr. John Willet et.al, in *Voices of Conscience: Poetry from Oppression*, eds H. Cronyn, R. McKane and S. Watts, Iron Press, 1995, pp. 23–4.

2   *A History of London*, Stephen Inwood, Macmillan, London, 1998, pp. 774–80.

3   'The British Museum Reading Room', in *Louis MacNeice: Collected Poems*, Faber & Faber, 1979.

4   *I Shall Bear Witness: The diaries of Viktor Klemperer 1933–41*, Weidenfeld & Nicolson, 1998.

5   *DBWG* 13, pp. 34–5.

6   *DBWG* 15, pp. 243–53.

7   *History of the Present: Essays, Sketches and Dispatches from Europe in the 1990s*, Timothy Garton Ash, Allen Lane The Penguin Press, 1999.

8   *A Concise History of Germany*, Mary Fulbrook, Cambridge University Press, updated edition, 1995, p. 138.

9   See 'Overwhelmed by their own fascination with "the ideas of 1933": Berlin's Protestant Social Milieu in the Third Reich', Manfred Gailus, *German History*, Volume 20, No. 4, 2002, pages 462–93.

10   *DBWG* 10, pp. 383–4.

11   *DBWG* 10, p. 385.

12   My view is that Bonhoeffer's life was marked by both continuity and change, and that Bethge's influential proposal that there were two major breaks in his life (from theologian to Christian, and later from Church to world) helpfully emphasizes developments in Bonhoeffer's approach, but can unhelpfully obscure continuities in his thought.

13   *Hitler: 1889–1936: Hubris*, Ian Kershaw, Penguin, 1998.

14   *A Concise History of Germany*, Mary Fulbrook, Cambridge University Press, updated edition, 1995, Chapter 6.

15   *Dietrich Bonhoeffer: A Biography* , Eberhard Bethge, Fortress, 2000, pp. 207–8.

16   Bonhoeffer's views on the 'Jewish Question' were much influenced by Martin Luther and retain features that, in light of the Holocaust, justly disturb some commentators. There is a body of literature debating Bonhoeffer and the Jews. It is useful to note that Bonhoeffer's experience of Judaism did not include any encounter in depth with Judaism as a living religion, but was mediated chiefly through the New Testament and Christian theology and history.

17   Quotation from 'The Social Message of the German Christians', in *The Church Controversy in Germany*, by Anders Nygren, Billing & Sons, 1934.

18   Gailus, art. cit., p. 483.

19   Gailus, art. cit., p. 474.

20   When in the early 1960s *The Sound of Music* was being filmed in the Austrian city of Salzburg the city council refused a request from the producers to put up Nazi banners in the city's main square saying that 'the people of Salzburg never supported the Nazis'. The producers got their way by threatening to use contemporary newsreel footage showing the enthusiastic welcome given by Salzburgers to the Nazi Anschluss of 1938.

21   See their correspondence in *Love Letters from Cell 92*, Harper Collins, London, 1994.

22   *Hitler: A Study in Tyranny*, Alan Bullock, Pelican, 1962, p. 735.

23   Mary Fulbrook, op. cit., p. 202.

24   *Plotting Hitler's Death*, Joachim Fest, Weidenfeld & Nicolson, London, 1996, p. 208.

25   Ibid., p. 342.

26   Ibid., pp. 3–4.

27   Ibid., p. 343.

3

Bonhoeffer's theological inheritance

The wish to be independent in everything is a false pride. Even what we owe to others belongs to ourselves and is part of our own lives, and any attempt to calculate what we have 'earned' for ourselves and what we owe to other people is certainly not Christian, and is, moreover, a futile undertaking. It's through what he himself is, plus what he receives, that a man becomes a complete entity.[1]

Bonhoeffer was thinking of the role of personal friendships in shaping him, but his comment is equally true of writers who had influenced him intellectually. Bonhoeffer was unique, yet he was also a product; of a family, as we have seen, of an educational system, and of key intellectual 'ancestors' whose work he tapped for the minerals with which to nourish his own ideas. Yet his roots in the loam of theological and philosophical traditions are not always visible. After Bonhoeffer qualified as a university lecturer he departed from many of the conventions of academic theology. He did not often use the technique of writing theology by discussing the work of other theologians. His did not use footnotes extensively. To Bonhoeffer, writing in difficult circumstances, against the clock or expecting imminent arrest, such practices may have seemed less crucial than they do to most scholars. Certainly Bonhoeffer read widely, as for example his extant notes for the *Ethics* show,[2] but the theology of others interested him less for its own sake than for the contribution it might make to thinking through the problems he faced. The importance of theological sources cannot simply be calculated by totting up how often he quotes them. Neither can we estimate the significance of a source simply by proving Bonhoeffer agreed with it. At least as important as the sources with which Bonhoeffer fundamentally agreed are those with which he fundamentally disagreed; the following discussions illustrate both source varieties.

When he died there were over 50 books on ethics in Bonhoeffer's possession as well as sections on ethics in broader theological texts or in collected works. To make this chapter manageable therefore each section discusses one 'book' written by four intellectual 'ancestors' with which Bonhoeffer was familiar: a translation of the Bible and three books. These discussions function like trenches, dug by an archaeologist across a far larger site in the hope of uncovering something of importance in a limited time. Whole books have been written on Bonhoeffer's relationship to just one of these sources (for example on Bonhoeffer and Luther). But while the choice of four ancestors – not three or five – is arbitrary; the choice of these particular four is not. Certainly, there were others who influenced Bonhoeffer's theological development – for example, Heidegger, Hegel and Dilthey and Barth – and I am not suggesting that the sources discussed here are the only important ones, merely that they are among the most important and that they serve to illustrate the ways in which awareness of sources can unlock the meaning of Bonhoeffer's writings.

Luther's Bible

The Reformer Martin Luther (1483–1546) had a greater impact on Bonhoeffer's theology than any other individual. Yet sorting out Luther's direct influence from that of the general milieu of Lutheranism that permeated German theology and culture and in which Bonhoeffer lived can be tricky. Bonhoeffer's teacher Karl Holl had contributed, with others,[3] to a renewed interest in Luther as a theologian and had included in his teaching a strong emphasis on Luther's ethics.

Yet a crucial point at which Luther exerts influence on Bonhoeffer has remained virtually unexplored: Bonhoeffer's reliance on the Luther translation of the Bible. Biblical translation involves theological decisions that interpret, often unconsciously, the meaning of a text. Consequently, Bonhoeffer's reliance on the Luther Bible involved the adoption at source of theological interpretations carried within Luther's translation. Bonhoeffer thought it was significant that he based his exegesis upon a German translation of the Bible: 'Anyone really concerned with the salvation of his soul', he said in 1935, 'has found that Luther's German version of Holy Scripture still best fulfils the demand for the presentation of the Gospel in a German way. Here is Christianity which is both present and German ...' (*NRS*, 305). For English speakers in the twenty-first century, with a great choice of Bible translations, it is hard to grasp the fact that the 'familiar Luther text' had no competitor as a vehicle of encounter with the Word of God.

What particular qualities are embodied in Luther's translation of the Bible? In an essay on 'Luther's German Bible' Heinz Bluhm highlights several features which begin to answer this question.[4] Bluhm attempts to encapsulate something of the 'singularly elusive quality' of Luther's rendering of the text in the vernacular. Luther's Bible was the first serious attempt in German to translate directly from the original languages. Luther worked from Erasmus's Greek New Testament of 1519. In 1517 however, while translating seven penitential Psalms, Luther's Hebrew was still insufficient for him to base his new rendering on the original language. But Luther's aim was not only to produce an accurate translation, but also a readable one. In his 'Open Letter on Translating' (1530) he wrote in defence against Papal attacks on his departure from the Vulgate that 'I wanted to speak German, not Latin or Greek'. His aim resulted in the 1531 rendering in which 'the Hebrew Psalter has virtually become a German Hymnal, actually reading in many places like original German sacred poetry'.[5] Bonhoeffer drew two conclusions from using Luther's Bible. He noted that 'translation itself is always fatal to any doctrine of verbal inspiration, as it is only the original text which is inspired' (*NRS*, 317). More than this, the '*Germanness*' of Luther's Bible enabled him to respond to the *German Christians*, who were seeking to reconstruct a set of 'German Scriptures', that it 'still best fulfils the demand for the presentation of the Gospel in a German way. Here is Christianity which is "both present and German"' (*DBWG* 14, 403).

In theological terms far the most important feature of Luther's translation was not the beauty of his language, but his 'rediscovery' of the theology of Paul. His reading of Paul permeated Luther's translation of the Bible. Luther's own interpretation of Paul was so decisive for him that it even functioned to an extent as a means through which an integrative unity could be imposed on the diverse theologies of New Testament writers. Luther's decision to re-order the books as they occur in the New Testament provides an illustration of this: by placing the letter to the Hebrews and the letter of James after the Johannine epistles in his translation Luther hoped to draw attention away from their strongly un-Pauline theology. More significant was Luther's idiosyncratic wording of crucial passages. The most notable of these is his insertion of the word 'alone' in Romans 3:28, which in Luther became 'justification is by faith *alone*'.[6]

Luther's translation of the Bible also embodied a further theological insight not discussed by Bluhm but crucial in the context of Bonhoeffer's theology in the Nazi context. Martin Luther insisted that the person of Christ was as much revealed in the Old Testament as in the New, and that the Old Testament was therefore equally the Church's Scripture. In his *Introduction to the Old Testament* (1545) Luther wrote that 'The ground and proof of the New Testament are surely not to be despised, and therefore the Old Testament is to be highly regarded'. This view underlay his commitment, paradoxical alongside his sharp distinction between Law and Gospel, to the unity of the Bible as God's Word. In his *Preface to the Psalter* Luther argued that 'The Psalter ought to be a dear and beloved book, if only because it promises Christ's death and resurrection so clearly, and so typifies his kingdom and the condition and nature of all Christendom that it might well be called a little Bible.' Luther's views of the relationship between the Old and the New Testament raise some difficult questions, for example about the way Christians have 'colonized' Jewish Scripture, or about reading into Scriptural texts Christian theological perspectives the original authors cannot have intended; similar questions are raised by Bonhoeffer's use of Old Testament texts (as we shall see, for example, in Chapter 5). For now, however, all I want to remark is the extent to which Dietrich Bonhoeffer adopted Luther's understanding of Scripture – its unity, its centrality for theology and the nature of its authority rooted in Christ – as his own. Very often Martin Luther is the most frequently cited source in what Bonhoeffer wrote. But even where Luther's influence is not made explicit, it is there, not least in Bonhoeffer's reliance on the Luther Bible. Three of the five books he published during his lifetime appropriate biblical texts for contemporary theological situations. He wrote extended essays on the Ten

Commandments; on the books of Ezra and Nehemiah; on the Psalms; on the biblical account of temptation and the Lord's Prayer. He wrote over 100 sermons and addresses on biblical texts and in Prison wrote that he read the Bible 'above all' (*LPP* 26). Bonhoeffer is unusual among twentieth-century German systematic theologians in using the Bible so much, and even more unusual in using the Old Testament as much as the New. Bonhoeffer's theological ethics are a commentary on the Luther Bible.

Kant's *Fundamental Principles of the Metaphysic of Morals*[7] (hereafter *Morals*)

Immanuel Kant (1724–1804) was the first major philosopher to write in the German language and the first of the modern era to earn a living as a professional academic. Perhaps because he was coining a new German philosophical vocabulary his writing style is notoriously opaque: 'there is no art in being intelligible', Kant wrote, 'if one renounces all thoroughness of insight' (*Morals*, p. 37). Kant stood at the confluence of two streams of Enlightenment thought. In one, Isaac Newton's (1642–1727) physics proposed a system of laws applying to space and time. In another, empirical philosophers such as David Hume (1711–76) argued that the only sure ground for knowledge was what our senses experience. Formerly, the study of the natural sciences, religion and philosophy had largely proceeded hand in hand; increasingly many sensed a conflict between scientific and religious forms of knowing. From Kant's perspective, religion and philosophy were in serious trouble. Science was based on experiment and observation or on Newtonian laws of the universe; in contrast, philosophy and religion seemed to make statements that were unfalsifiable and unproveable. Religion supposed that every person possessed a free will. Science supposes that laws govern events in the physical world: things don't 'just happen', they happen because they have a cause, and science could show what those causes were. Religion, including ethics, needed 'free will' to make sense; but if science was right that causal explanations can be found for all human behaviour then ethics wastes itself in discussing choices that people actually do not have. More importantly still, in such a world what role was left for God? These were the problems that Kant set out to tackle.

Kant's *Fundamental Principles of the Metaphysic of Morals,* published in 1785, fitted morality into a far grander philosophical system. It is called *metaphysic* of morals because it is a 'pure' form of philosophical analysis rather than applied to concrete moral problems or derived from observation of human behaviour, for example within anthropology (*Morals*, 38). Kant argued that the world is made up of what he calls 'phenomena' (the way things appear to a perceiving subject) and 'noumena' (the way things actually are in themselves). Kant agreed with earlier philosophers that we only know the world as it is presented to us via the medium of our senses, and concluded that the belief that the mind can really know things (phenomena) in themselves is an illusion. Yet Kant did not despair of our ability to know things or make judgements. Kant distinguished two types of 'judgement' – 'synthetic' and 'analytic'. A judgement is analytic if it makes sense all on its own, for example 'a father is male' or 'a square has four sides'. All other judgements – for example 'all men are arrogant', or judgements about empirical matters such as 'copper conducts electricity' – are synthetic: the truth of a 'synthetic' statement, that is, is not self-evident but rests on a 'proof' not contained in the statement/judgement itself. Kant continued that judgements are also either *a priori* (true by nature of the terms used and the rules governing their use, and thus knowable in advance of their application) or *a posteriori* (true according to how things are observed in the world and knowable only after an event as knowledge contingent upon experience). He concluded that the judgements we make are of three types. They can be analytic and *a priori*; synthetic and *a priori*, or synthetic and *a posteriori*. For Kant, knowledge of morals is of the second type, synthetic (i.e. it is not self-evident) and *a priori* (i.e. made up of laws knowable in advance). He therefore describes moral reason as 'practical reason' because it derives its principles from a mind's own rational nature, not from examples drawn from the experience of the senses (*Morals*, 35), and not from (pure) theoretical reasoning (*Morals*, 11–12). By describing morals as *a priori* Kant means that all moral statements must be timeless, unchanging, and the same for all human beings whatever culture they belong to and whatever circumstances they are in.

But if morals are not based on experience, on what are they based? Kant asserts that '[n]othing can possibly be conceived in the world, or even out of it, which can be called good without qualification, except a Good Will' (*Morals*, 17). The 'Good Will' is the supreme good and condition of every other good. Obeying one's own good will, therefore, rather than pursuing personal happiness, is the goal of morality; in other words doing good and being happy do not necessarily coincide and one's personal inclinations can be a poor guide to moral action. The important thing is not to do what one wants to do, but to do what one should. Kant describes this as *duty*: 'love, as an affection, cannot be commanded, but beneficence for duty's sake may' (*Morals*, 24). But from where does duty derive its content (i.e. how may duty be a duty to do something specific, rather than remaining abstract only)? Kant answers: 'from the maxim by which it is determined'. A maxim, he continued, is a subjective principle of the will (*Morals*, 24). Kant did try to bridge the gap between the subjective will and the universal principles of morality. It is crucial that any maxim I act on should be one I want everyone to act on. Take promises: if I make a promise I later regret, I might wish to break my promise because that is what suits me. But, asks Kant, what would happen if everyone behaved like that? Promises would become completely worthless, and society would crumble. If I want others to keep their promises to me, I must keep my promises to them and the rule I set myself, therefore, should be one I wish everyone to follow, that is, it ought to be a universal law. This means a moral imperative is a *categorical imperative*. Imperatives can be hypothetical, e.g. 'if you eat lots of fruit, you will be more healthy'. But hypothetical imperatives only tell us to do something good as a means to something else. Kant argues that a moral imperative must be categorical: 'It concerns not the matter of the action, or its intended result, and what is essentially good in it consists in the mental disposition, let the consequence be what it may (*Morals*, 44).' Of this type there is only one: 'Act only on that maxim whereby thou canst at the same time will that it should become a universal law' (*Morals*, 49). The universal, moral law is thus clearly independent of any particular social order for Kant. Monogamy may be practised in one culture, polygamy in another, but if Kant is correct only one or the other can be morally right. The categorical imperative also implies freedom: its 'you ought' implies the possibility of disobedience. This freedom entails two important consequences: firstly, it is important that other people are treated by us not as means, but as moral ends in themselves: 'a man is not a thing, that is to say, something which can be used merely as a means, but must in all his actions be always considered to be an end in himself' (*Morals*, 58). This freedom implies, secondly, that each reasoning and moral subject is autonomous, and this is exactly Kant's conclusion, which he correctly perceived to be an original discovery in ethics:

Looking back now on all previous attempts to discover the principle of morality, we need not wonder why they all fail. It was seen that man was bound to laws by duty, but it was not observed that the laws to which he is subject are *only those of his own giving*, though at the same time they are *universal*, and that he is bound to act in conformity with his own will ... (*Morals*, 61)

Kant's philosophy was revolutionary. The poet and essayist Heinrich Heine (1797–1856) mischievously expanded Kant's own flattering comparison of the effects of his philosophy with Copernicus's revolutionary theories: 'Formerly reason, like the sun, went round the world of appearances and tried to cast light on it; but Kant makes reason, the sun, stand still, and the world of appearances turns around it and is illuminated as it enters the realm of this sun.'[8] The centre of Kant's 'moral universe' Heine hints, is not God but the reasoning individual. If all we know are appearances we cannot know God in himself any more than we can know anything in itself. By demolishing all arguments for the existence of God, Heine writes, Kant 'has stormed heaven ... the Supreme Lord of the world, unproved, is weltering in his blood'.[9] Yet after this tragic loss of the possibility of knowing God comes farce as Kant goes on to argue that while God cannot be proved by pure reason, He can be still be believed in by means of practical reason. Heine's caricature is satire, but like most satire there is truth in it. Kant 'allows' God's existence, and with God Kant permits ethics; but we are left with a suspicion that restoration has been achieved by philosophical sleight of hand.

Kant was still a dominant force in philosophy and ethics when Bonhoeffer was a student. As well as reading Kant's own books, many of the ethical textbooks from which Bonhoeffer read took Kant as the central authority.[10] Yet Bonhoeffer was from his earliest student period keen to challenge Kant's dominance in Protestant ethics, and for two key reasons. Firstly, Bonhoeffer believed, Kant had been mistaken in placing the reasoning mind of the individual at the centre of the study of ethics. For Bonhoeffer human beings meet the world not only as individuals but as members of communities of people: of nations, of classes, of families and of churches. If Kant's ethics neglected the communal nature of human life, they also largely neglected the Christian God. 'God', to be sure, was present in Kant's philosophy and ethics, but Jesus Christ and the Holy Spirit were not. This made it all the more extraordinary that Kant's thought had become the default basis for Protestant theological ethics. Bonhoeffer therefore took Kant seriously, as we shall see in the next chapter, but used his philosophy as an anvil against which to hammer out a more distinctively Christian ethics. He achieved this in part using two very diverse sources: the writings of Søren Kierkegaard and Friedrich Nietzsche.

Kierkegaard's *Fear and Trembling*

No theologian teases his readers more than Søren Kierkegaard (1813–55), though his playfulness both endears and frustrates. One of the 'games' Kierkegaard plays with us is his use of pseudonymous authorship for many of his books. For example, *Fear and Trembling* (*FT*) was published (in 1843) under the pen name 'Johannes *de silentio*'. Using pen-names was not, for Kierkegaard, an attempt to preserve anonymity: it was a literary device rather like the creation of a narrator in a novel that enabled him to step into the shoes of a fictional character and explore thoroughly and consistently what that character might think. It cannot, therefore, be assumed that Johannes' thinking in *Fear and Trembling* represents what Kierkegaard thought, or indeed that it does not, since fictional narrators do sometimes resemble their authors. But the strategy enabled Kierkegaard to create viewpoints he did not necessarily hold himself, but which he felt were necessary in order to make progress in a wider debate. A second 'game' Kierkegaard plays is to use unconventional means of communicating philosophy and theology, in particular through telling or retelling stories. Such is the case in *Fear and Trembling*, in which the biblical story of Abraham and Isaac is told and retold from several perspectives that open up alternate ways of understanding what was taking place.

Bonhoeffer discussed *Fear and Trembling* at the beginning of his career in *Sanctorum Communio* and at the end of his career was still commending it to his fiancée.[11] In a paper given at Union Seminary Bonhoeffer includes Kierkegaard in a list of genuine Christian thinkers with Paul, Augustine, Luther and Barth.[12] Most significantly Kierkegaard's ideas were important to Bonhoeffer in framing the terms of his book *Discipleship*, in which, as we shall see in Chapter 6, the contrast between cheap and costly grace, derived from Kierkegaard, is central. Yet Bonhoeffer rarely discusses Kierkegaard's writings at any length and the precise role and significance of Kierkegaard for Bonhoeffer is therefore moot. In particular, commentators are not agreed whether Bonhoeffer had grasped Kierkegaard's thought thoroughly or superficially.[13] My purpose in this section is to draw out of *Fear and Trembling* an issue that I believe is fundamental not only to that phase of his life when Bonhoeffer wrote *Discipleship*, but to his theological ethics as a whole: this is the concept of a '*teleological suspension of the ethical*'.

A starting point for the discussion that Kierkegaard stages in *Fear and Trembling* is Kant's view that all human beings owe a categorical obedience to moral duty. Kant believed that it was absurd to imagine that God might command something that was unethical. From Kierkegaard's point of view what this would mean, if true, is that duty to God is no more than duty to ethics and that human beings owe nothing to God except the duty embodied in morality. But what, Kierkegaard asks, if sometimes God directly commands an individual to do something that breaks the moral law? Just this situation arises in the story of God's command to Abraham to sacrifice his son Isaac in Genesis 22. Kierkegaard imagines several possible explanations for this extraordinary story. When he raised his knife to kill his son did Abraham pretend to be a vicious idolater so that Isaac would be spared the thought that the true God had ordered his death? Did he go through events on the mountain and thereafter lose all joy because he could not forget what God put him through? Did he sin by thinking God was prepared to order him to sacrifice Isaac? Did Isaac lose faith?

For Kierkegaard, this is not a remote classroom dilemma. He believed that the church to which he belonged in Denmark had cheapened faith by transforming the Gospel into an empty cliché-ridden and this-worldly piety. Imagine a churchgoer, Kierkegaard writes, who hears Abraham praised in a Sunday sermon and prepares to imitate him. When the preacher hears of his plans he shouts 'loathsome man, dregs of society, what the devil so possessed you that you wanted to murder your own son?' when all the man is preparing to do is what the preacher had urged in his sermon. God demands everything; but in contemporary church life, paraphrasing W. H. Auden, it never crosses our minds he means exactly what he says. Yet there is more to *Fear and Trembling* than a call to commit oneself more fully to God. Genesis 22 teaches that there is a 'monstrous paradox' in Abraham's life that philosophy is quite unable to account for. At face value, what we see in Abraham is 'infinite resignation' to the will of God. Yet if that is all that is to be found in Abraham, he is no more than a tragic hero. Probe deeper, Kierkegaard suggests, and Abraham goes a crucial step beyond resignation: not only did he resign himself to God's command to kill his son, he trusted that somehow God's promise would still be fulfilled. Infinite resignation 'is the last stage before faith' but is not itself faith. Faith, Kierkegaard says, goes beyond resignation to believe 'on the strength of the absurd, on the strength of the fact that for God all things are possible'. What Kierkegaard presents here is a fundamental critique of philosophy from the basis of faith. Either Kant is right and Abraham was a man who murderously disobeyed his ethical duty, or Abraham truly is an exemplar of faith. It is also a critique of theology that wants to sell faith 'at a bargain price' – to denude faith of its absolute and absurd demands.

This account of faith raises three closely related ethical problems. The first is: Is there a teleological suspension of the ethical, that is can moral laws ever be suspended for the sake of a goal or end beyond ethical duty? 'The ethical', Kierkegaard explains, summarizing Kantian ethics:

> as such is the universal, and as the universal it applies to everyone, which can be put from another point of view by saying it applies at every moment. It rests immanently in itself, has nothing outside itself that is its *telos* [end, purpose] but is itself the *telos* for everything outside, and when that is taken up into it, has no further to go.[14]

If this really were the end of the matter then one could clearly not surrender one's duty to ethics. Yet faith, Kierkegaard suggests 'is just this paradox, that the single individual is higher than the universal', not only in spite of the fact that this is absurd, but 'on the strength of the absurd' (FT 84–5). Abraham does not obey a higher ethical duty in preparing to sacrifice Isaac: in 'his action he overstepped the ethical altogether, and had a higher *telos* outside it, in relation to which he suspended it' (FT 88). This raises the second ethical dilemma: Is there an absolute duty to God? Kantian ethics suggests that duty to ethics *is* duty to God. But for Kierkegaard our duty to our neighbour is not at all the same thing as our duty to God. This does not mean that a person with faith ceases to have an obligation to love her neighbour, but means that sometimes love of God may cause us to act towards our neighbour in ways that contradict our ethical duty – just as Abraham was prepared to contradict his paternal obligations to Isaac in obedience to God. A third ethical dilemma again follows: Was it ethically defensible for Abraham to conceal his purpose from Sarah and from Isaac? Ethically, the answer is clearly 'no'. But if he was to obey God then Abraham had to remain silent: he *cannot* speak and still obey. Abraham's silence breaks the rules of ethics and obeys the command of God. (Is this the reason Kierkegaard employs the pen-name Johannes *de silentio*?)

It is tempting to make a connection at this point between Abraham's obedient silence and Christ's silence on the cross. Yet Bonhoeffer's theology will not permit such a connection, and the reason why reveals both where Bonhoeffer draws on Kierkegaard, and where he departs from him. Kierkegaard's proposal for a 'teleological suspension of the ethical' drives a wedge between Christian obedience and philosophical ethics. It distinguishes, as Kant did not, obedience to moral law and obedience to God. Abraham, whom Kierkegaard characterizes as a 'knight of faith', discovered that in certain rare circumstances God demands we act in ways that are unethical. Bonhoeffer in his belief that Christian 'ethics' is a critique of all other ethics took up this insight. We shall meet this idea later in Chapters 5, 6 and 7. Yet Bonhoeffer disagreed with Kierkegaard in a second, equally important respect. Kierkegaard's *Fear and Trembling* proposes that the individual is higher than the community. The consequence of this is that in the duty to love one's neighbour it is not God we meet, but merely the neighbour, since our duty to God can cause us to 'suspend' our ethical obligation to our neighbour. For Bonhoeffer, the choice between God and neighbour was false because God meets us in our neighbour. It was true, for Bonhoeffer, that Kierkegaard had correctly turned away from Kant in presenting a critique of philosophical ethics from the biblical point of view: but Kierkegaard had wrongly followed Kant in making the individual central to ethics. For Bonhoeffer, as we shall see in the next chapter, individuals meet God in community, not in isolated individualism.

Towards the end of his life Karl Barth, reflecting on the strong influence of Kierkegaard on his early writings, said he considered Kierkegaard 'to be a teacher into whose school every theologian must go once. Woe to him who has missed it! So long as he does not remain in or return to it.' On this at least, Bonhoeffer followed Barth's lead.

Nietzche's *Beyond Good and Evil*

Dietrich Bonhoeffer may seem to be an unlikely successor to Friedrich Nietzsche (1844–1900). Nietzsche's reputation is of a man at odds with Christianity; a prophet of meaninglessness and chaos, whose literary creations declared the death of God. Yet in one striking respect Bonhoeffer's theological ethics rest on Nietzsche's foundations: both of them attempt to re-conceive human life *Beyond Good and Evil*.[15] Nietzsche imagined 'a music whose rarest magic would consist in this, that it no longer knew anything of good and evil'.[16] For his part Bonhoeffer asserted, in a deliberate theological appropriation of Nietzsche's atheistic idea, that 'The knowledge of good and evil seems to be the aim of all ethical reflection. The first task of Christian ethics is to invalidate this knowledge' (*E* 3).

Bonhoeffer owned several volumes of Nietzsche and a collected works.[17] Within his *Ethics* he cites several of Nietzsche's works as well as using phrases such as 'Ecce Homo' and 'twilight of the gods' that draw on a common European heritage but are nonetheless reminiscent of Nietzsche. Though elsewhere he makes a number of passing and positive references to Nietzsche, Bonhoeffer's only extensive discussion of him outside the *Ethics* occurs in an address given in Barcelona where, more than ten years before he repeated these themes in the *Ethics*, Bonhoeffer argued for an ethic 'beyond good and evil' linked with Nietzsche's name.

Beyond Good and Evil, published in 1886, was Nietzsche's sixth and last book of aphorisms. He regarded it as a critique of modernity and, according to its subtitle, as a 'Prelude to a Philosophy of the Future'. Nietzsche thought that to understand ethical terms such as good and evil it was important to understand their origins. Originally, he thought, what was 'good' was the same as what was 'noble', while 'bad' was associated with the 'simple' people, who Nietzsche disparagingly calls 'the herd'. Faced with the 'master morality' which suppressed them, the 'herd' struck back by creating a morality of its own in which the highest values of the master morality – strength and nobility – became the greatest evils in the morality of the weak. In this way Nietzsche suggests that there is malign intent in a morality of good and evil: 'Moral judgement and condemnation is the favourite form of revenge of the spiritually limited on those who are less so' (*Beyond*:219, 130). Between these two moralities the contrast looks like this: 'The noble type of man feels *himself* to be the determiner of values, he does not need to be approved of, he judges "what harms me is harmful in itself", he knows himself to be that which in general first accords honour to things, he *creates values*' (*Beyond*:260, 176). On the other hand, there is the 'slave morality':

> The slave is suspicious of the virtues of the powerful: he is sceptical and mistrustful, *keenly* mistrustful, of everything 'good' that is honoured among them – he would like to convince himself that happiness itself is not genuine among them. On the other hand, those qualities which serve to make easier the existence of

suffering will be brought into prominence and flooded with light: here it is that pity, the kind and helping hand, the warm heart, patience, industriousness, humility and friendliness come into honour – for here these are the most useful qualities and virtually the only means of enduring the burden of existence. (*Beyond*:260, 178)

And here, Nietzsche draws the crucial conclusion that:

Slave morality is essentially the morality of utility. Here is the source of the famous antithesis 'good' and 'evil' – power and danger were felt to exist in evil, a certain dreadfulness, subtlety and strength which could not admit of contempt. (*Beyond*:260, 178)

It is, in Nietzsche's distinctive phrasing, a morality of *ressentiment*.

It should already be clear that Nietzsche's imperative to go 'beyond good and evil' does not make for nihilism of the more banal kind. Aware he might be misinterpreted he spells out that 'as for the dangerous formula "beyond good and evil" with which we at any rate guard against being taken for what we are not: we are something different from *"libres-penseurs"*, *"liberi pensatori"*, *"Freidenker"* [i.e. free-thinkers], or whatever else all these worthy advocates of "modern ideas" like to call themselves' (*Beyond*:44, 54). His proposal, Nietzsche insists, is constructive not destructive, and though described as an attempt to live beyond the old morality (*Beyond*:262, 182) it is not an attempt to live without morals. This is because 'that which is done out of love always takes place beyond good and evil' (*Beyond*:153, 85). Nietzsche does not advocate the destruction of morality but the 'transvaluation of all values', the freedom for the élite moral agent to become the creator of his own morality (and being a notorious misogynist he did mean 'his' and not 'her' morality. For Nietzsche good and evil are not opposites – the erroneous belief of a slave morality – but are two sides of the same coin. He recognized that the distinction between good and evil does not represent the natural or ideal state of humankind. His solution was to deny the concept of sin. For Nietzsche, crudely put Eve and Adam had got it right; the fruit of the knowledge of good and evil did belong to them, and his proposal for ethics involved opening Eden to them once again in order that they might truly become like gods, free from the superficial sensation of guilt.

Bonhoeffer's focus on Nietzsche's ethics rather than on his philosophy is unusual in a theologian. For Bonhoeffer, Nietzsche is not to be thought of as an enemy of Christianity, but rather as something of a prophet. Of course for Bonhoeffer the solution to the problem of good and evil is not to assert that human beings are gods, but to turn to God become Man in Christ Jesus. In this context Bonhoeffer concludes that:

> It is not, as Nietzsche supposed, because it arises from these dark motives that judgement is wrongful; judgement is evil because it is itself apostasy, and that is the reason why it brings forth evil in the human heart ... 'Judging' is not a special vice or wickedness of the disunited man; it is his essence, manifesting itself in his speech, his action and his sentiment. (*E* 17)

Though Nietzsche provides the insight and the language prompting Bonhoeffer's ethic 'beyond good and evil', ultimately Nietzsche is as much the subject of Bonhoeffer's critique of secular ethics as Kant. To maintain an anthropocentric ethic in any form, according to Bonhoeffer, is to maintain an ethic after the Fall. Because we are creatures, not creators as Nietzsche supposed, we cannot be *übermenschen*, 'supermen', but are always simply ordinary human beings limited by time and space. This remains true even though the *moral* limitations of humanity are radically redescribed by God's commitment to creation in becoming Man in Jesus. This is certainly an irresolvable disagreement between Nietzsche and Bonhoeffer. Yet when, in *Ecce Homo*, Nietzsche comments 'When I wage war against Christianity I am entitled to do this because I have never experienced misfortunes and frustrations from that quarter – the most serious Christians have always been well disposed towards me';[18] it may well be, as Jörg Rades commented, that Nietzsche had theologians like Bonhoeffer in mind.

Provisional conclusion

Karl Barth suggested tentatively that Bonhoeffer was 'an impulsive, visionary thinker who was suddenly seized by an idea to which he gave lively form, and then after a time he called a halt (one never knew whether it was final or temporary) with some provisional last point or other'.[19] Visionary, yes; but perhaps not as impulsive as Barth thought. The value of tracking some of the roots of Bonhoeffer's thinking is partly to make better sense of what he himself came to think. But it can also help us to appreciate that what may appear to be intellectual kite flying exercises are, on closer inspection, securely earthed in Bonhoeffer's knowledge of intellectual traditions. The discussions in this chapter will begin to pay dividends when we explore Bonhoeffer's own writings in the next and succeeding chapters.

Notes

1   *LPP*, p. 150. Jörg Rades, a graduate student in Scotland, died in April 1989. In the months before he died, with many drugs in his system and writing in a second language, Rades wrote several essays exploring the influence of several key thinkers on Bonhoeffer. They remain among the best essays of their kind. This chapter is indebted to him.

2   *Zettelnotizen für eine 'Ethik'*, ed. Ilse Tödt, Chr Kaiser Vlg, Munich, 1993, publishes Bonhoeffer's notes towards his book on *Ethics*. They show that even where a reference to a source is not given in the text of his drafts essays, he has paid full and proper attention to them.

3   See *Martin Luther: German Saviour*, James M. Stayer, McGill-Queen's University Press, Montreal, 2000, for a study of Luther interpretation in Weimar Germany.

4   'Luther's German Bible', chapter VIII of *Seven-Headed Luther*, ed. P. N. Brooks, Clarendon, 1983.

5   Bluhm, op. cit., p. 183.

6   Luther's interpretation of Paul has been challenged by much recent scholarship, which suggests that the sharp contrast between Law and Gospel was Luther's theological construct and is not borne out by careful study of Paul in his historical and sociological setting.

7   *Fundamental Principles of the Metaphysic of Morals*, Prometheus, New York, 1998.

8   'On the History of Religion and Philosophy in Germany', in *Selected Prose*, Heinrich Heine, Penguin, Harmondsworth, 1993, p. 273.

9   Ibid., p. 276.

10   To cite one example, in 1926 Nicolai Hartmann, Professor of Philosophy at the University of Berlin, published his three volume *Ethics*. A copy of it, annotated by Bonhoeffer, exists. It would not be too gross an exaggeration to describe it as a commentary on Kant's ethics.

11   *Love Letters from Cell 92*, Dietrich Bonhoeffer and Maria von Wedemeyer, Harper Collins, 1994, p. 154.

12   *DBW* 10, p. 432.

13   See the debate between David Hopper, Paul Matheny and Daniel Hardy in the International Bonhoeffer Society *Newsletter*, issues number 44 (May 1990) and 45 (October 1990).

14   *Fear and Trembling*, S. Kierkegaard, Penguin, 1985, p. 83.

15   Cited by Julia Watkin in *Kierkegaard*, Geoffrey Chapman, London, 1997, p. 100. Bonhoeffer shared with Nietzsche a desire to break free of the hegemony of Kantian ethics, and in particular used Nietzsche to shore up his conviction that there are no universal moral rules. This, in spite of Nietzsche's assertion that 'the Protestant pastor is the grandfather of German Philosophy', and that 'Kant's success is merely a theologian's success'.

16   Friedrich Nietzsche, *Beyond Good and Evil*, London, Penguin, 1973, Part 8, no. 255, p. 169 (hereafter *Beyond* 8:255, 169).

17   Details in the *Nachlass*, p. 220.

18   *On the Genealogy of Morals/Ecce Homo*, F. Nietzsche, Vintage, 1989, p. 233.

19   Letter from Karl Barth to P. W. Herrenbrück, 21 December 1952, in *World Come of Age*, ed. R. Gregor Smith, Collins, 1967, pp. 89–90.

4

Self, community and revelation: building blocks of ethics

Bonhoeffer's decision to write his doctoral dissertation on the Church seems far less strange now than it did in 1925. Today, the role the Church plays in shaping Christian life is a central concern of the discipline and practice of ethics. But in 1925 Protestant theology and ethics was focused far more on the individual. Above all this approach was embodied in Adolf von Harnack who, his great age notwithstanding, was a towering authority of liberal Protestant theology, the pope 'of the Protestant professorial curia'.[1] Von Harnack's method was based on the conviction that true theology must distinguish between the essentials and the inessentials of Christianity, between its kernel and its husk. This meant stripping away what he considered to be the outer layers of theological specu-lation using 'scientific' historical tools. Historical theology, von Harnack believed, could establish what Jesus said and did and what became of his original message in the early history of the Church. Proper historical study of Christian theology, von Harnack believed, meant that *anyone*, albeit with professional scholarly guidance, could arrive at an authentic form of Christianity free of the extra-neous additions of both Jewish theology and Greek philosophy. In practice, this amounted to distinguishing a 'genuine' gospel of Jesus from that of later Church dogma. Jesus' gospel of the kingdom of

God, von Harnack thought, was *not* directed to the church, or indeed to any other form of community, but to the individual:

> The kingdom of God comes by coming to the individual, by entering into his soul and laying hold of it. True, the kingdom of God is the rule of God; but it is the rule of the holy God in the hearts of individuals; *it is God himself in his power*. From this point of view everything that was dramatic in the external and historical sense has vanished; and gone, too, are all external hopes for the future. Take whatever parable you will, the parable of the sower, of the pearl of great price, of the treasure buried in the field – the word of God, God himself, is the kingdom. It is not a question of angels and devils, thrones and principalities, but of God and the soul, the soul and its God.[2]

Von Harnack's approach seemed to many the highest possible expression of Protestant theology with its emphasis on the direct encounter of God and the individual, free of the authority of the Church.

Bonhoeffer studied Christian Doctrine with von Harnack in 1924 and from 1924 to 1926 participated in two more seminars with him. Yet even in his teens, Bonhoeffer was reaching beyond Berlin and the historical approach to theology that dominated there towards the light of *dialectical theology*. The term 'dialectical theology' was beginning to be attached to a loose knit circle of theologians, including Karl Barth, Emil Brunner, Friedrich Gogarten and Rudolf Bultmann, concerned with holding together a scholarly, rational and 'scientific' study – of the Bible, church history and religious psychology – with a lively Christian faith. The discipline of theology, they maintained, must move 'dialectically' between these poles holding the apparently contradictory demands of rational reflection and faith in paradoxical tension. Bonhoeffer aspired to a theological method that would enable him to integrate the methods of the Berlin faculty and those of dialectical theology. This method-ological break with his own faculty was reflected in his choice of subject matter for his two university dissertations. Von Harnack and his followers viewed the Church as a barrier to the authentic encounter of the individual and the gospel rather than as its vehicle. Where the Church attracted their attention at all it was treated merely as historical data. Bonhoeffer wanted to examine the Church using scholarly tools, such as sociology and social philosophy, but also to regard the Church from the perspective of faith as the body of Christ – a premise that lay outside the disciplines of history and sociology.

Bonhoeffer's doctoral dissertation was written in 1927 and published in 1930 under the title *Sanctorum Communio* (the holy community); his second dissertation, *Act and Being*, written to qualify him as a university lecturer, was completed in 1930 and published a year later. Both dissertations are situated in conflicts and debates from which theology has long since moved on. This might suggest that they have little if any contemporary interest – and very probably if Bonhoeffer had not come after his death to be widely regarded as an outstanding Christian thinker his academic dissertations would be no better remembered than the scores of other dissertations published in Berlin at the time, which is to say hardly at all. For contemporary students of theology, reading these books is therefore often justified simply because they form the basis of Bonhoeffer's later work, and this is certainly the case: part of my argument in this book is that a trajectory can be traced in Bonhoeffer's ethics that begins with these two dissertations and ends with Bonhoeffer's prison letters. But in this chapter I want to open up two contemporary ethical debates to which these early books contribute irrespective of their value in illuminating later developments in Bonhoeffer's theology.

Making links between Bonhoeffer's dissertations and contemporary moral problems is far from straightforward. The highly technical language and style of both dissertations sometimes makes them difficult to follow. They discuss philosophical and theological sources that are very demanding and some of which are now unfamiliar to all but the most expert scholars. It is easy to see why the dissertations take the form they do: one commentator on *Sanctorum Communio* points out that even Bonhoeffer-enthusiasts cannot avoid the 'sad truth (all too evident in this instance) that academic dissertations are not written to enlighten the public but to impress a faculty committee'.[3] Certainly, in writing his two academic dissertations, the young Bonhoeffer was not aiming primarily at clarity and elegance of expression; a contemporary reader of *Sanctorum Communio* told Bonhoeffer's uncle 'your nephew still has to learn German'.[4] Seventeen years after he presented *Sanctorum Communio* to his Faculty examiners Bonhoeffer himself had come to feel abashed at the form his theology then took and wrote to his young fiancée '[Y]ou're twenty years old! I am thoroughly ashamed to recall how ignorant I was at that age, and how replete your own life already is, by comparison, with experiences and tasks of the utmost importance. I still believed then that life consisted of ideas and books, and wrote my first book [i.e. *Sanctorum Communio*], and was, I'm afraid to say, inordinately proud of it.'[5] Bonhoeffer was young when he wrote *Sanctorum Communio* and *Act and Being*: and even if he exhibits a level of maturity within them far in excess of his years (and he does), at this stage of his development he can be forgiven for leaving some threads untied and some elements not fully resolved. Yet such difficulties can too easily become excuses for ignoring these remarkable and precocious early writings.

The two debates outlined below are both important; classical Greek philosophy energetically considered how individuals and society fit together, and how being good fits in with doing good things. The relation of the individual to society has been arguably the central debate in English-speaking political ethics during the last twenty years. My interest in these particular debates – rather than in other equally important discussions in contemporary ethics – arises from the central role these same debates play in Bonhoeffer's early theology to which this chapter attends. I am not looking in current ethics for theories or models with which to interpret or to critique Bonhoeffer's theology, though that might be both possible and useful. I want to ask what issues are raised within these debates and to see how Bonhoeffer's early theology might help us to think through them.

Self and community[6]

At the height of her power the British Prime Minister Margaret Thatcher gave an interview to a women's magazine on the philosophy that lay behind her political programme. The magazine led its report of the interview with the Prime Minister's statement that there was 'no such thing as society'. Her critics, who took it as evidence that the Conservative Party led by Mrs Thatcher was wilfully intent on social disintegration, rampant self-interest and individualism, promptly seized upon this catchy phrase. Whatever view one takes of the merits of Thatcher's political philosophy, we may better understand her meaning if the phrase is restored to its context in the interview. There is no such thing as society, she said, but there:

> are individual men and women, and there are families. And no government can do anything except through people, and people

must look to themselves first. It's our duty to look after ourselves and then to look after our neighbour.[7]

Society, she believed, is not best thought of as an abstract thing-in-itself, but as a living structure of individuals, families, neighbours and voluntary associations (among which, presumably, she included churches). This political philosophy, at least in theory, should lead to a downsizing of the role of the state in people's lives. It is a view that von Harnack would have recognized and affirmed: states, he thought, are not redeemed by Jesus' gospel, individuals are.

Margaret Thatcher did not originate this view of the relation between individuals and society; it is a fundamental tenet of a wider tradition of postwar liberal political theory. Following the Second World War political philosophical debate had stagnated. In 1972 the philosopher John Rawls kick-started a new phase of political thinking with his book *A Theory of Justice*,[8] which wittingly or unwittingly provided the basis for the 'new right' political programmes of both Margaret Thatcher and Ronald Reagan. Rawls asserted that 'the self is prior to the ends which are affirmed by it', that is in both moral and political life the individual moral agent exists prior to any social identity she may also have. It is primarily as an individual that she makes moral choices and has moral rights, such as the right to own property. Even if she aligns herself with a moral community, such as a church, her primary moral identity does not originate in the shared values of that community, since her ability to choose to belong precedes her actual belonging.

Those who believe that moral identity is primarily centred in community articulate a diametrically opposing view. Prominent among advocates of 'communitarianism' is the philosopher Alasdair MacIntyre. MacIntyre insists that morality is acquired by being part of a community in which moral traditions are embodied and passed on. People are formed morally by the stories told by particular communities, stories that are lived out in moral practice. So much is this the case that when community is fragmented – as is the case in much contemporary life – morality in any meaningful sense ceases to exist. In short morality *is* community tradition, and without community there can be no morality. By and large recent theological ethics has been in profound sympathy with the communitarian views held by MacIntyre – who indeed resources part of his argument by reference to the theology of Thomas Aquinas. Christian theology, in which retelling the 'stories' of the Bible plays a central role, has found it natural to maintain that narrating stories in the context of the

Church can shape a person's moral life. In particular this resonance with communitarianism has found a focus in 'narrative theology', a vogue term describing theology that reflects on and out from the role of story in the Church. Significantly for our purposes, Stanley Hauerwas, a prominent advocate of attending to the role of narrative in the Church, utilizes the 'narrative character of Christian convictions' in developing a vigorous theological ethics:

> The nature of Christian ethics is determined by the fact that Christian convictions take the form of a story, or perhaps better, a set of stories that constitutes a tradition, which in turn creates and forms a community. Christian ethics does not begin by emphasizing rules or principles, but by calling our attention to a narrative that tells of God's dealing with creation ... it is crucial for us ... to see that it is not accidentally a narrative.[9]

MacIntyre and Hauerwas offer an attractive vision of community life, but their subordination of the moral individual to the moral community raises awkward questions (which they respond to far better than my brief summary of their arguments might suggest). Both agree that since morality is deeply embedded in particular moral communities, there can be no such thing as a universal morality, as Kant supposed. But how then, are we to distinguish between 'good' moral communities and 'bad' ones? Obviously, where the moral codes of two communities conflict, they cannot both be right. The Nazis believed firmly in a national 'community', the German *Volk*: on what basis may I assert that its views and practices were morally repugnant? Hauerwas would say that I can know this because I belong to another community, the Church, which embodies a radically different ethic rooted in God's love. But is this not better characterized as an irresolvable conflict of two rival moralities? MacIntyre also recognizes the nature of the problem and responds by arguing that in a healthy society in which different, incommensurable (moral) systems are in apparently irresolvable conflict a debate may arise in which one system turns out to be superior in more adequately accounting for difficulties with its own and other traditions.[10] Another dimension to the problem surfaces when we consider that in practice most people belong not to one but to several moral communities. I am a member of a Church, but I am also a member of a family, a member of a university, a member of a political party and a member of a nation. What happens when the moralities of these communities conflict not simply with each other, but within me? Does Hauerwas' way of putting things suggest that I belong solely to the Church, and that this community should properly be not only my Church, but also, in a sense, my family, university, political 'community' and nation?

The debate about the relationship between self and community has remained a vigorous one in both political philosophy and in theological ethics. In our turn towards Bonhoeffer's early writings this contemporary debate can help furnish us with questions to which we are still looking for answers nearly eighty years on:

- What is a community?
- Which comes first (in ethics) – the individual or the community?
- Is the Christian community (i.e. the Church) different from other kinds of human community?
- Is there a way of resolving conflicts between the Church and other moral communities?

Doing good and being good

How I tell a good person from a bad one is not a new conundrum in ethics. Plato debates the question 'how do we recognize a just person?' in his *Republic* and in *The Nichomachean Ethics*; Aristotle, Plato's recalcitrant pupil, takes up the same problem. The question has been a component of ethics ever since. One aspect of this discussion concerns the relationship between deeds and character: is a person good because he performs good acts or because he is good in himself? Aristotle's answer was that character was crucial. He argued that 'we become just by doing just acts, temperate by doing temperate acts, brave by doing brave acts'.[11] That is, goodness does not come naturally but by consciously forming habits of good behaviour, which Aristotle terms virtues.

For the greater part of Christian history, under the influence of classical philosophy, Christians also maintained that character is at the heart of ethics. In the thirteenth century the theologian Thomas Aquinas transposed Aristotle's philosophy into Christian theology, thereby reiterating the importance of virtue and character in Christian ethics. But in the sixteenth century this emphasis on character was disrupted in the Protestant theology of Martin Luther and John Calvin. Luther was suspicious of the idea that people, under their own steam, could develop good character; human beings were naturally too sinful to be good. Luther believed that by considering the laws given by God in the Bible it becomes painfully clear that humanity is rotten to the core. Yet God does not leave humanity in this Fallen state; for by the law God turns human lives towards the need for His grace and forgiveness. Luther conceded a second use of law in restraining human sinful actions through the exercise of legal discipline by secular ruling authorities. John Calvin agreed with all this, but went a step further. He argued that beyond the first two uses of the law outlined by Luther, God's law is able to teach, encourage and inspire the believer to do good. God's commandments, Calvin says, were not cancelled by God's gift of forgiveness in Jesus Christ, but interpreted anew by his life and work.

The Reformation thus set two theological cats into the pigeon loft of virtue ethics. Luther called into question human ability to be good without divine grace. Calvin pressed the question of if and how God commands the believer to act according to His law. But if what matters is obedience to God's commandments, then is the significance of one's personal virtue and character not relativized? As a consequence of Luther's and Calvin's related but distinct theologies there exists in Protestant ethics a sometimes-unresolved tension between an emphasis on human sinfulness (and the doctrine of salvation by faith alone) and the requirements of direct obedience to God's law. In modern times Protestant theologians have tended to follow Luther and Calvin in their rejection of ethics based on virtue and character. However, recently there has been a remarkable recovery of virtue ethics. Philosophers such as Alasdair MacIntyre, Iris Murdoch and Martha Nussbaum, and theologians such as Stanley Hauerwas, have argued that the parlous state of contemporary moral discourse and practice can be revivified by a return to virtue-based ethics, in which what we mean by 'good' in phrases like 'good community' or 'good person' refer to prized qualities of life or prized features of moral character. Contemporary theological ethics manifests this tension in the contrast between ethics in which obedience to (God-given) rules, laws or commandments is central; and ethics conceived as an ongoing process of character formation in which one is shaped by practices such as worship, prayer, Bible reading and community life. It is a contrast between moral agency conceived as right choices and good character; between obedience and virtue; between act and being.

This current debate raises further questions that we can usefully hold in mind when reading Bonhoeffer's early writings:

• How, in Christian ethics, should the relationship between good acts and being good be conceived?

- What should I *do*? ('What must I do to inherit eternal life?' Mark10:17).
- Who should I *be*? (What kind of person should I be?)

Sanctorum Communio

The structure of the Church as a community, Bonhoeffer begins, can only be understood when theology employs the tools of social philosophy and sociology. When these tools are used, it becomes clear that 'all the basic Christian concepts ... "[P]erson", "primal state", "sin", and "revelation" can be fully comprehended only in relation to sociality' (*DBW 1* 21), not only the social relations of human beings with each other, but the sociality of human beings with God. Social philosophy deals with the social relations presupposed by empirical community, that is community as it is experienced and observed, rather than in theory alone. Sociology is the study of the structures of human social formations in order to understand how people and groups behave. Yet to realize the insights of social philosophy for a theology of the Church means adopting a presupposition which social philosophy and sociology do not themselves adopt, namely that the real structure of the Church can only be grasped by those to whom its inner reality is revealed by Christ. This is because 'the nature of the church can only be understood from within, *cum iraet studio* [with passionate zeal], never by nonparticipants' (*DBW 1* 33). What Bonhoeffer seeks, in other words, is not to examine personhood and personal relations, or community *as such*, but to unlock a Christian concept of personhood and community.

In dialogue with social philosophy Bonhoeffer arrives at a Christian understanding of personhood expressed in strikingly ethical terms. For Bonhoeffer, each individual discovers what it means to be a human person when she accepts that those she meets constitute barriers or limits to herself, i.e. when the 'I' realizes that her own needs and desires are not all that matter, since the 'you' encountered has needs and desires of their own. A proper sense of human identity is 'created in the moment of being moved – in the situation of responsibility, passionate ethical struggle, confrontation by an overwhelming claim; thus the real person grows out of the concrete situation' (*DBW 1* 49). Primarily this takes place when we come face to face with God as the ultimate Other, whose divine person transcends my limited human person. But, by analogy, each person we encounter demands a similar realization that our personhood is bounded by social and ethical relationships. The social and ethical character of the individual means that properly speaking we do not exist as human beings in isolation, but only in accepting our responsibility to the other in our face to face encounter with him. Bonhoeffer describes this as a meeting of the concrete 'I' with the concrete 'You'. Ethics begins with the realization that I can never *be* you; that the social barrier between us is at the same time an ethical barrier. This barrier is not best conceived as a chasm, but rather as a point of resistance between the will of the 'I' and the will of the 'You'. The self is self-encapsulated, turned in on itself; in short the self is selfish! It is not the otherness of the other, however, that results in its isolation – the otherness of the other is her God-given individuality. Rather, it is sin which isolates each individual and prevents community. Bonhoeffer recognizes that in speaking of an 'uncrossable' boundary between I and You, he risks implying that, however responsible I may *feel* for You, I am in the last resort isolated from You by the barrier between us. It is at this point that Bonhoeffer makes a claim that becomes fundamental to the argument of the whole book. Though one human being cannot of her own accord cross this barrier, yet

> *God or the Holy Spirit joins the concrete You; only through God's active working does the other become a You to me from whom my I arises. In other words, every human You is an image of the divine You.* (*DBW 1* 54–5, Bonhoeffer's italics)

Genuine ethical responsibility becomes possible, Bonhoeffer claims, when God assumes the place of the 'You' in the I–You encounter, making it possible for the I to recognize the needs of the other.

The *theological* origins of Bonhoeffer's argument lie in the biblical story of Adam's original state of unbroken community with God. When Adam sinned at the Fall, his relationship with God was fundamentally altered, but so also was his social relationship with Eve. The concepts of person and community must be interpreted theologically in the light of this biblical account of original unbroken community, of the Fall, and of restored unity – or salvation – in Christ. But how, Bonhoeffer asks, are 'person' and 'community' related in this context? A Christian understanding of person supposes that a person has a spirit. The spirit in a person is the self-consciousness and self-determination that holds a person together as a unified whole, and is expressed in acts of thought, will and feeling. Such acts are only evident in social exchanges, and can become explicit in language. In short, human spirit in its entirety is woven into the interaction of the I and the You; 'this is the essence of spirit, to be oneself through being in the other' (*DBW 1* 73). This community of persons is broken at the Fall and can only be restored in Christ. But which matters most in this: the individual or the community? 'In theological terms,' asks Bonhoeffer, 'does God intend by community something that absorbs the individual human being into itself, or does God intend *only the individual*? Or are community and individual both intended in their distinctive signifi-cance?' (*DBW 1* 76). Bonhoeffer refuses to treat this question as an either/or decision: community or individual. Instead, he suggests that a community, just as much as an individual, is held together as a unified whole by a (human) spirit around which it coheres: '*We maintain that community can be interpreted as a collective person with the same structure as the individual person*' (*DBW 1* 77). This collective personality or spirit of the community is not ordered hierarchically in relation to the individual spirits that make it up, as if individual spirit was subordinate to the collective spirit. Rather, the distinct personality of the community, which to be sure transcends its individual component parts, only exists because of the individual spirits that make it up. God, Bonhoeffer believes, does not see us as isolated individuals but as a human community in which, nevertheless, individuality is not dissolved in a homogeneous collective whole. Borrowing from Hegel's philosophy, Bonhoeffer terms this community spirit 'objective spirit' – to be set alongside the 'subjective spirit' of the individual. When two or more individuals form a community, this 'objective spirit' comes into being as a 'new' personality that brings to community its historical and communal identity and continuity in space and time. The sense in which a community with an 'objective spirit' has a 'body' is complex. Obviously, a community does not have a 'single' body in the same sense as an individual does: a community is not an organism. Yet there is a sense in which communities, such as a family or a nation are *tangible* realities. (Thomas Hobbes's 1651 political treatise *Leviathan* pictured a great 'collective' being, made up of countless individual faces that made up the body of the nation with the King as its head.) The sense in which the Church is spoken of as 'the body of Christ' is unique, certainly, but in this sense it is not completely different to other forms of human community. Not all groups of people that have 'objective spirit', however, are communities. Bonhoeffer distinguishes between a society and a community. A society, he suggests, is oriented towards a *goal* or purpose (which is not necessarily a bad thing); while a community is oriented towards its self-preservation. Because of such differences, only a community has a personality in the way Bonhoeffer means it.

The interweaving of the individual and the communal illuminates Bonhoeffer's account of sin, in which the culpability of the individual and of all humanity is closely connected. Original sin can hardly be thought of in terms of genetic inheritance or biology, as if children and those with mental disability are 'sinful' in the same way as fully developed adults. Bonhoeffer's formulation of the relationship between an individual sinful act and the collective sin of all humanity is to state that: 'When, in the sinful act, the individual spirit rises up against God . . . the deed committed is at the same time *the deed of the human race* (no longer in the biological sense) *in the individual person*' (*DBW 1* 115). Bonhoeffer's claim is that as a single individual can sin, a community can sin. A community is ethically responsible, like a person, and expresses itself ethically when an individual, such as a spokesperson, office holder, leader, or member acts on behalf of the whole community. In this way a community such as a married couple, a nation, or the human race, can sin. This helps to explain why, in the Bible, the call of God's prophets is invariably to the people of God rather than to the individual. In this sense, communities can be extremely varied: at the smallest end of the scale a marriage is a community, at the largest end the human race is a community.

Only now that the ground has been prepared does Bonhoeffer turn, more than a third of the way into his book, to the *Sanctorum Communio*, the holy community of the Church. Paul wrote to the Corinthians that 'as all die in Adam, so all will be made alive in Christ' (1 Corinthians 15:22). In the Church-community being-in-Adam is replaced by being-in-Christ. But this only means that the Church is free of sin in an eschatological sense, that is, as God's promise and the Church's hope. Christians sin. For this reason the 'real' Church should not be confused either with the visible religious community called church, or with the Kingdom of God. The 'real' Church is a reality of revelation visible only with the eyes of faith. This belief, i.e. in the Church, distinguishes Christianity from other religions, Bonhoeffer asserts, in which community is not an essential. He adds, in a somewhat idiosyncratic exegesis, that the New Testament teaches that each individual congregation embodies the totality of the Church – indeed, where an individual Christian is present, the whole Church may be said to be present. This community exists through Christ's action, in which the brokenness of Adam is superseded by Him as the new Adam, who is both the cornerstone of the Church, and is at all times really present in it, since the church is Christ's body and has Him as its collective personality. Bonhoeffer expresses this 'real presence' in a term that effectively sums up the whole of the book's argument: 'Christ existing as church community' (*DBW 1* 141).

The existence of Christ in the Church community is *invisible* in the sense that the perfected body of Christ is promised at the end of time, but is *visible* in worship and in Christians' working-for-each-other. Bonhoeffer accepts that the ethical imperative to love one's neighbour is not confined to Christian theology. However, 'the reality of love is nevertheless present only in Christ and in his church-community' (*DBW 1* 167). He explains this demanding statement on the basis that '*Christian love is not a human possibility*' (*DBW 1* 167–8), it is not a matter of sympathy or humanitarianism, or compassion, or, in a different meaning of love, eroticism. Christian love is possible only through faith in Christ. As a *Christian*, I love You my neighbour, not because it benefits me or gives me pleasure, but because I experience in You God's claim upon me. This does not mean that I love God in You, rather than loving You in yourself and for Your own sake; rather, only God's Spirit enables me to overcome the ethical barrier between us *in order that* I can come to love You as you really are. My love for You is an expression of my intention to embrace God's will and purposes for you, and to do so without limits. Where such love is realized, that is in God, can community truly come into being. This community is a way of *being* with each other in a community appointed by God; and it is a way of *acting* together in which members of the community act with and for each other. This mode of 'action-for' Bonhoeffer calls the principle of 'vicarious representative action' or deputyship [in German S*tellvertretung*, literally 'standing in place of'], an idea to which Bonhoeffer would return in his *Ethics*.

In spite of Bonhoeffer's frequent insistence that he describes the Church in concrete rather than in abstract ways, his description has seemed to some to be 'idealized' in the sense that it bears little resemblance to the experience most of us have of the church as a flawed community of flawed individuals. The sociologist Peter Berger has noted that in *Sanctorum Communio* '[T]he empirical is retained as an element of definition. But one looks in vain through the pages of *Sanctorum Communio* for any utilization of empirical data concerning the relationship of religion and society. In other words, despite Bonhoeffer's definitions, his dialogue is actually one between social philosophy and dogmatic theology, both operating on levels of abstraction safely removed from the harshness of empirical data.'[12] This is fair up to a point, as Bonhoeffer does not refer to sociological studies of the church as it is observed. Yet he is well aware of the imperfections in practice of members within the church community: 'there are some who are strong and others who are weak, some who are honourable and others who are dishonourable, some who are, from an ethical and religious perspective exemplary and others who are inferior', to say nothing of the many social differences that exist within the church (*DBW 1* 206). The unity of the church then, clearly does not mean that everyone is equally good (or equally bad); but is there any means of distinguishing 'true' believers from nominal believers? Bonhoeffer answers that while the Kingdom of God is made up of all those who are predestined by God as members of the church community, the church that is visible to us in the world is comprised, through infant baptism, of those who are *potentially* members of the Kingdom of God. It is in the sacrament of the Lord's Supper that those who are serious about submitting to the rule of God gather together. The church-community of spirit has its source in Christ's gift of Himself in bread and wine, which symbolically expresses the gathering of individuals into community.

Four questions answered

What is a community? For Bonhoeffer, a community can be thought of as a collective person with an 'objective spirit' that comes into being when two or more individuals come together to form a 'new' collective self capable of thought, intention, feeling and action. Most groups of individuals commonly called 'communities' are in reality merely societies formed around a goal or task, and are therefore impermanent. Social philosophy and sociology, Bonhoeffer claims, help to identify and describe 'community', but are unable to recognize the Church-community, which is only visible with the eyes of Christian faith and which is, theologically speaking, unique in relation to all other forms of community. A community can be as small as a community of two (e.g. a marriage) or large as all human beings (in the community of the human race).

In answer to the question 'which comes first: the individual or the community?' Bonhoeffer asserts that '[I]n God's eyes, community and individual exist in the same moment and rest in one another'

(*DBW 1* 80). The choice 'individual or community' is, for Bonhoeffer, a false one; it is, rather a case of *both* individual *and* community. The community does not take priority over the individual and the individual does not take priority over the community.

But how is the church-community different from other forms of community? For Bonhoeffer, the church-community shares common features with other forms of human community. Most significantly the church-community, though it lives in anticipation of holy perfection, remains in the present a sinful community that shares in Adam's (fallen) humanity. Yet the church alone is 'Christ existing as church-community'.[13] Community is essential to Christianity, Bonhoeffer maintains, as it is not essential to other religions.[14] This does not mean that true community only takes place in the observable community of the local congregation, since the Kingdom of God is not identical with the church. But only in God can the barrier that exists between I and You be transcended; only in God is community truly possible.

This raises the question of how, in communities other than the Church, the ethical barrier between individuals may be crossed to allow *them* to become 'collective personalities'. Presumably, the same God who makes it possible to overcome the ethical barrier between individuals – and therefore makes community possible – is also able to overcome barriers between communities and to enable a community of communities. The description of the 'other' (the 'You') as *different* to the 'I' – which Bonhoeffer derived from his reading of social philosophy – might provide a model for the social–ethical relations of collective personalities (i.e. of different moral communities) as much as it does the relations of individuals.

Act and Being

Imagine a friend, someone you *know* well: how do you know what he is like? How do you know who he is? Perhaps you think you know him because of how he treats you (e.g. because he is kind) or because he tells you about his history or his opinions. Perhaps you think you know him because of something he has done (e.g. you might think he is thoughtful because he gave you an appropriate birthday gift). Fine: but do any of these things lead you to think you *really* know him completely? Put positively, is the element of mystery in human relationships one of the things that makes them worth investing ourselves in?

In all human relationships, there is an element of risk, an element of trust, and a dimension that lies open to the future. In some respects knowing God is similar to knowing a friend; for example, we can never say we 'know' God, if what we mean by that is that we have apprehended everything God *is*. Our relationship with God, like our relationship with a friend can never be complete because if it is healthy we are constantly learning new things. But knowing God also has characteristics that are unique. While we have a lot in common with a friend (we are both human beings) God is not the same as us (for example God is uncreated and we are created). If we truly know anything about God, we know that God is greater than the capacity of our imagination (or if you prefer, our mind) to grasp God. But does this mean that we cannot really know anything about God at all? Immanuel Kant expressed this problem with particular clarity and force. He was interested primarily in the possibility of philosophical knowledge that transcends the bounds of experience, but what he said of philosophy had profound implications for human knowledge of God too. Kant thought that human knowledge was limited to the way things 'appear' to the mind, to what he called phenomena. Things in themselves, what he called noumena are, he said, thinkable (imaginable) but not actually knowable. Knowing God was, for Kant, a special case of this teaching. Kant believed that one cannot say 'I know God exists' and mean by it that we know God as God is in himself. Yet he did not think this necessarily meant that saying 'I know God exists' is a lie. Take out a penny from your pocket; now 'set alongside it' an *imaginary* penny. The 'real' penny and the imaginary penny are very different: you can touch one and not the other, for example. But one can still say some things about the imaginary penny that are as 'true' about it as they are of the real penny: for example there is only *one* real penny and there is only *one* imaginary penny. Similarly, we can say some things that are 'true' about God, even if our minds cannot really know God as God is in Godself. Kant called his theory 'transcendental idealism'. Bonhoeffer thought that Kant's 'transcendental idealism' was largely responsible for the crisis in philosophy and theology that in *Act and Being* he wanted to resolve. *Philosophically*, the problem is epistemological (i.e. it has to do with theories that explain questions like 'how do I know something?' and 'how does a subject know an object?'). *Theologically* this is the problem of revelation (i.e. 'in what sense is God disclosed to humanity, and how is this possible?' 'in what sense are theological concepts based on revelation *true*?').

Bonhoeffer characterized this problem as 'an attempt to come to an agreement about the problem of act and being' (*DBW 2*, 25). Is God known in the act of faith, a moment in which God gives Godself? Or does God somehow *exist* in his revelation, so that in it we know God's being? Bonhoeffer believed that Barth's view (remember he was writing in the late 1920s) was closer to the former, that is to an act-based understanding of revelation that emphasized the freedom of God *from* his revelation in order to preserve God's ultimate *aseity*, God's infinite qualitative difference from humankind. Though Bonhoeffer respected the basic orientation of Barth's theology he suspected it retained elements of Kant's erroneous view, as he saw it, that God cannot *really* be apprehended by the human mind. At the same time Martin Heidegger was pioneering a philosophical revolution that challenged Kant's approach by reopening a question, long ignored by philosophy, about the nature of *being* (the technical term is *ontology*). In Heidegger's brilliant, if incomplete, analysis of being – in German '*Dasein*' ('being there') – he argued that the essence of human *Dasein*, lies in an individual's capacity to reflect on his own *existence*. Human *Dasein*, that is, does not have a fixed nature; 'its essence lies in its always having its being to be, and having it as its own', so that our 'being' depends on our understanding of it. Bonhoeffer wanted to see how the Barthian theological revolution (with its emphasis on God's freedom in revelation) and the Heideggerian philosophical revolution (with its fresh approach to ontology) could be brought together. 'In other words', he wrote, the question is how 'the meaning of "the being of God in revelation" must be interpreted, theologically, including how it is known, how faith as act, and revelation as being, are related to one another and, correspondingly, *how human beings stand in light of revelation*' (*DBW 2* 28). This 'theoretical' question of how act and being cohere has cash value in the relation between an individual's act of faith – von Harnack's overriding concern and that of liberal Protestantism – and the being of the Church-community[15] of Christ, which Bonhoeffer had described in *Sanctorum Communio*.

In the first part of *Act and Being* Bonhoeffer deepened his examination of the alternatives established by Kant's transcendental idealism and Heidegger's ontology. Kant's transcendental idealism, Bonhoeffer asserted, had been taken to an extreme by later idealist thinkers. While Kant thought that the objects of knowledge, i.e. the world, are in reference to me, later idealists believed more extremely that the world actually 'comes about' through my apprehension of it.

Thus, it is more accurate to say there are, in philosophy, not two but three alternative understandings of how the transcendent is apprehended by the mind: 'Transcendental philosophy regards thinking to be "in reference to" transcendence; idealism takes transcendent being into thinking; and, finally, ontology leaves being fully independent of thinking and accords being priority over thinking' (*DBW 2* 60). Bonhoeffer wanted, without altogether dismissing them, to move beyond all three approaches because '[T]hinking is as little able as good works to deliver the *cor corvum in se* [the heart turned in upon itself – Luther's phrase] from itself' (*DBW 2* 80). The problem was *how* to do this; his solution was to return to the ideas developed in his doctoral dissertation by looking at how the Church interprets revelation as both act *and* being.

In *Sanctorum Communio* Bonhoeffer had argued that the Church can only be properly understood from within; now he transposed that insight into epistemology by asserting that 'only those who have been placed into the truth can understand themselves in truth' (*DBW 2* 81); that is only those who approach knowledge from *within* (God's) revelation will understand the extent to which human beings, on their own, are incapable of true knowledge. Revelation is not something that the human mind abstracts from its investigation of the world: it is God's gift. Bonhoeffer understood, therefore, what Barth intended by maintaining that God is not bound to anything, not even to the historical record of his revelation in the Bible. If we think revelation is *contained* in the Bible, there is a danger that we transform God's free Word into something static that is at the disposal of every individual who takes the Bible into her hand. But Bonhoeffer could not accept Barth's insistence that revelation is an event, an act of God who gives – or withholds – Godself freely. This was where 'transcendentalism is lurking' in Barth's theology.[16] For Bonhoeffer, this was simply not the best way to put things. In reply, he proposed that:

> In revelation it is not so much a question of the freedom of God – eternally remaining within the divine self, aseity – on the other side of revelation, as it is of God's coming out of God's own self in revelation. It is a matter of God's *given* Word, the covenant in which God is bound by God's own action ... God is free not from human beings but for them. Christ is the word of God's freedom. God *is* present, that is, not in eternal nonobjectivity but – to put it quite provisionally for now – 'haveable', graspable in the Word within the church. (*DBW 2* 90–1)

To expand this 'provisional' explanation and to balance Barth's – and Kant's – one-sided account of act, Bonhoeffer looked at revelation from the perspective of being. In what sense, he asked, does God *exist* in revelation – that is, how exactly is God 'haveable' in God's Word? Already within theology Bonhoeffer discerned three possible explanations of the *being* of God in revelation; but in none of them did he find what he was looking for. One explanation speaks of God existing within theological doctrine. The problem with this, however, is that even if the doctrine concerned is 'true', for example the teaching that God is gracious, there is every danger that God becomes tied down in doctrine within a human system of belief. If God really did exist in doctrine, faith would no longer be God's free gift, but a human possibility – an act of the mind and the will which grasps God by understanding a doctrine and by then choosing to assent to it. A second view of 'revelation as being' is to understand it as a religious experience. This view teaches that 'God is found in my experience, understandable and subject to classification within the human system of experiences' (*DBW 2* 104) as if God were required to reveal Godself according to the quality of my spiritual life. Bonhoeffer suspected that here too there was a sleight of hand, for one may have religious experience without a genuinely life-transforming encounter with God's existence. Finally, revelation may be conceived as embodied in an institution. Bonhoeffer gives two examples: Protestants who maintain that the Bible is verbally inspired by God; and Roman Catholics who believe the Church to be a divinely instituted embodiment of revelation. In these institutional forms of revelation God *is* again bound up and at the disposal of human beings, as if when one affirms the verbal inspiration of Scripture or joins the (true) Church, God *must* be revealed to one in the words of Scripture, or in the authority of the Church's teaching office. In these three caricatures Bonhoeffer effects potentially devastating critiques of contemporary religion. God's creatures, Bonhoeffer insists, cannot take hold of and smother God's existence. God is free, and God's existence will remain remote unless 'God takes hold of human beings and turns them around' (*DBW 2* 106). This revelation takes place not in the Church considered as an institution, but in the Church where it is 'understood to be constituted by the present proclamation of Christ's death and resurrection – within, on the part of, and for the community of faith' (*DBW 2* 110). In the community of the Church God gives Godself to human individuals by setting their being in relation to Christ's. Where human being is in relation to Christ knowing too takes place in faith. Theological truth, Bonhoeffer argues, is only 'haveable' in the Church.

73

The full implications of Bonhoeffer's conclusion for philo-sophical and theological epistemology were profound. In the final part of his thesis Bonhoeffer began to unpack his attempt to unify act and being in relation to Paul's teaching that human being is 'in Adam' and 'in Christ'. For Bonhoeffer, Paul's characterization of human being 'in Adam' was both a richly ontological and biblical way of expressing human sinfulness. Luther's axiom was that we may only know that we are sinners *by faith*; Bonhoeffer understood by this that only though God's revelation can human beings *know* they are sinners. Paul's being 'in Adam' was identical with Luther's *cor corvum in se* – the heart turned in on itself in sin. Such sin is not only a violation of God's law; it is a denial of the true human *being* in God's image and likeness for which we were made. This truth disrupts any understanding of sin in terms of particular sinful acts, of specific sins committed in particular moments. If that is really all sin means, then becoming sinless would be relatively easy: one would simply need to stop committing sinful acts. But if sinful acts arise from sinful *being* – from being 'in Adam' – only the Saviour can restore being human to the wholeness of being 'in Christ'. The greater part of *Act and Being* was spent clarifying the questions at the heart of early twentieth-century theology. In the last few pages Bonhoeffer's writing style changes gear as he begins to point out directions in which answers to those questions may be found.

Three further questions answered

How, in ethics, should the relationship between good acts and being good be conceived? For Bonhoeffer, the answer does not take the form 'either/or', but 'both and'. What one *does* makes up who one *is*; but likewise, who one *is* determines what one does: 'Thus, in Adam act is as constitutive for being as being is for act; both act and being enter into judgement as guilty' (*DBW 2* 146). If it is the case, 'in Adam', that act and being cannot be uncoupled, what is the case 'in Christ'? For the Christian, Bonhoeffer continues, in the Church community the promise of a future new being in Christ is realized, for '[I]n faith the future is present . . . the human being "is" in the future of Christ – that is, never in being without act, and never in act without being' (*DBW 2* 159), 'always act, because it is being; always being, because it is act' (*DBW 2* 161).

There is nothing that an individual can do to realize this new being ('What must I do to inherit eternal life?' (Mark 10:17)), for '[H]uman beings are "there" for and by means of Christ': this is the mystery and gift of faith. The only thing one may do is to seek Christ, for nothing may be achieved by seeking to find one's own new being. In answer to the question 'Who should I *be* (what kind of person should I be)?' Bonhoeffer reiterates Jesus' demand that the disciple should be like a child. 'To-let-oneself-be-defined by means of the future is the eschatological possibility of the child. The child (full of anxiety and bliss) sees itself in the power of what "future things" will bring, and for that reason it can only live in the present' (*DBW 2* 159). The theological clue to this is given in the 'problem' of infant baptism, in which the child, unable consciously to reflect on itself, is nonetheless graced with the promise of God. The mature adult who is in Christ is recalled by her baptism into childhood, a call that can only be understood as an eschatological promise. Infant baptism constitutes a direct act of God, an *actus directus* in contrast to the act of reflection, the *actus reflexus*; for the true act of faith can never be conscious, but only ever a direct act of God. After many complex twists and turns, Bonhoeffer concludes *Act and Being* with great lucidity: 'It is the new creation of those born from out of the world's confines into the wideness of heaven, becoming what they were or never were, a creature of God, a child' (*DBW 2* 161).

Notes

1 *The Identity of Christianity*, Stephen Sykes, SPCK, 1984, p. 127.

2 *What is Christianity*, Adolf von Harnack, Williams & Norgate, 1912, pp. 57–8.

3 'Sociology and Ecclesiology', Peter Berger, p. 54 in *The Place of Bonhoeffer,* ed. Martin E. Marty, SCM, 1963.

4 *Dietrich Bonhoeffer: A Biography*, E. Bethge, Fortress, 2000, p. 167.

5 *Love Letters from Cell 92*, D. Bonhoeffer and M. Wedemeyer, Harper Collins, 1994, pp. 184–5.

6 In this section I am indebted to chapter 10, 'Self and Community', pp. 257–96, in *Politics Theology and History*, Raymond Plant, Cambridge University Press, 2001.

7 *Margaret Thatcher: The Downing Street Years*, Margaret Thatcher, Harper Collins, 1993, p. 626.

8 *A Theory of Justice*, John Rawls, Clarendon Press, Oxford, 1972.

9 *The Peaceable Kingdom*, Stanley Hauerwas, SCM, 1984, pp. 24–5.

10 See *Three Rival Versions of Moral Enquiry*, Alasdair MacIntyre, Duckworth, 1990.

11 *The Nichomachean Ethics*, Book İI:1, Aristotle, OUP, 1986, p. 29. This passage is cited by Bruce C. Birch and Larry L. Rasmussen in *Bible and Ethics in the Christian Life*, Augsburg, Minneapolis, 1989, p. 42.

12 Berger, art. cit., p. 59.

13 Bonhoeffer generally uses the word 'Gemeinschaft' for 'community' and 'Gemeinde' to mean the 'church community'. The somewhat ugly conjunction 'church-community' used by the translators of the *Dietrich Bonhoeffer Works* is an attempt to distinguish between these two kinds of community. However, the German word 'Gemeinde' can be translated as 'church', 'local congregation', 'parish' or 'community', depending on the context, and so can sometimes refer to worshipping believers, and sometimes to the whole 'community' – those who practise Christianity and those who do not – within the parish boundary.

14 The claim is rather rash! Bonhoeffer was virtually ignorant about other religious communities except through what he had read.

15 See note 13 above.

16 The accuracy of Bonhoeffer's portrayal of Barth's views is hotly debated.

5

The Fall: the origin of
Christian ethics

Dietrich Bonhoeffer's 1932/33 lectures on the first three chapters of
Genesis were formative for his theological ethics. This was the
period in which, Bonhoeffer would write in 1936, he discovered the
Bible and became a Christian. Also in 1933 Adolf Hitler became
German Reich Chancellor, changing the course of world history and
with it the direction of Bonhoeffer's life. What connections can be
made between these events – between Bonhoeffer's 'discovery' of
the Bible and his opposition to Nazi misrule? In this chapter I
explore this question in relation to *Creation and Fall*. In these
lectures Bonhoeffer realizes what has previously been implicit in his
theology: that reading the Bible and following Christ make a real
difference to the way the Christian lives in the world.

In reading Bonhoeffer's lectures I want to raise two sets of
questions. The first set of questions concerns the way that myths in
general, and the myth of the Fall in particular, can function as
commentary on contemporary moral or political concerns. The
seventeenth-century English poet John Milton can help us to open
this question out. Bonhoeffer's exegesis of creation and Fall was
given in Berlin against a vivid political backdrop. Even if he did not
intend the lectures as political commentary, the capacity of the Bible
to address the situation that he and his student audience now faced
can hardly have failed to interest Bonhoeffer. To what extent and in
what ways does Bonhoeffer's telling of the myths of creation and

Fall serve as commentary on the political crisis that developed around him? By reading Bonhoeffer's exegesis of creation and Fall alongside his more overtly political writings from this period, I hope to show something of Bonhoeffer's political theology.

A second set of questions flows from this first and concerns how Christian ethics is situated in relation to moral and political debate at the broadest public level. Such questions are stimulatingly explored by Stanley Hauerwas in his Gifford lectures of 2000/01 (published under the title *With the Grain of the Universe*)[1] which present a robust argument for the distinctiveness of Christian ethics. Hauerwas does this in part by means of a dialogue with Reinhold Niebuhr's social ethics. Bonhoeffer – who had been a less than slavish student of Niebuhr's in New York – likewise distinguished Christian ethics from all other ethics, but did so by means of the story of the Fall. It is through exegesis of Genesis 1–3 that Bonhoeffer articulates the view that Christian ethics stands apart from all other ethics and is a critique of all other ethics. A lot is at stake in this debate: is all ethical conversation a single activity in which Christians participate and for whom the *effectiveness* of Christian participation in society is the measure of its worth, as Niebuhr maintained? Or are Christian ethics really unique, in which case Christians are in the world but shaped by values and practices that distinguish them sharply from prevailing social mores, the only proper measure of which is not what impact their way of life has but the extent to which it witnesses faithfully to Christ?

John Milton, poetry, politics and the Fall

The biographical parallels between John Milton and Dietrich Bonhoeffer are few, but striking. Both lived through periods of political turmoil and war; both were considerable scholars; both were patriots committed to sharing the fate of their nation; both were imprisoned; both were thoroughgoing Protestants, though Milton was a heterodox Arminian and Bonhoeffer an orthodox Lutheran; both wrote poetry, though one was better at it than the other; Milton defended regicide and Bonhoeffer defended tyrannicide. But for my purposes it is not their biographies, but their respective treatments of the Fall that justify a comparison.

The struggle between England's King and England's parliament that took up the better part of John Milton's maturity occasioned the most vigorous political debate in English history. For a brief period all political options were open, from the divine right of kings, to the levelling of all ranks of people; from a society based on the individual ownership of property to one based on the common ownership of land and wealth. Some took a radical view of the Bible: the Digger Gerard Winstanley thought 'it matters not much' whether the Bible stories were true or not.[2] But in much of this revolutionary debate the Bible in general and the story of the Fall in particular was used as a vehicle of political conversation. The Bible was appealed to as justification for contrasting and competing political points of view. The story of the Fall was, for example, used to account for the need for private property, for the origins of social inequality, and for the necessity of the institutions of the state and of marriage.

In his account of *Milton and the English Revolution* Christopher Hill rehearses this context to explain the choice of the Fall as the subject of John Milton's *Paradise Lost* and *Paradise Regained*; but he also goes one step further. In both poems, Hill hypothesizes, 'Milton is grappling with problems set by the failure of God's cause in England'.[3] It was not simply that the doctrine of the Fall was integral to contemporary political discussion of private property, social inequality, of the state and of the family – all topics on which Milton had written before he began the poem cycles – but that by mid-1660, when he was under way with *Paradise Lost*, other avenues of political activity once open to him had been closed. Active as a political pamphleteer and as Cromwell's correspondence secretary, Milton was a steadfast propagandist of the Revolution. So on the eve of the Restoration in 1660 his previous proximity to power made overt political writing hazardous. Writing poems about the Fall allowed Milton to express political views with a chance that he would escape prosecution. Yet, Hill continues, the story of the Fall was not merely a *convenient* vehicle for Milton; it was also inspirationally *appropriate*. Milton believed the Bible to be true both as history and as allegory. The Fall of Adam recorded not only the origins of humankind, but illuminated the moral defects of the English in the 1650s. Adam served not only as forerunner of Christ, but as the prototype for the fallen leaders of the Revolution: the leaders of the English Commonwealth of 1659–60 were, for Milton, re-enacting 'as macabre farce the tragedy of the Fall'.[4] Adam expresses Milton's disillusioned viewpoint of English collective guilt:

Him after all disputes
Forced I absolve: above all my evasions vain

And reasonings, through mazes, lead me still
But to my own conviction: first and last
On me, me only, as the source and spring
Of all corruption, all the blame lights due.
(*Paradise Lost* X, lines 828–33)

The myth of the Fall proves, in the poetry of John Milton, to be a highly flexible means of interweaving theology and politics. It was not only that retelling a biblical story enabled Milton to escape the censor, but that the qualities in this particular myth seemed so obviously to account for central features of human sociality.

None of this would surprise Wendy Doniger who in the *The Implied Spider*[5] explores the relation of politics and theology in myth. Myth, Doniger believes, is a tool that can be used in a variety of ways, including both theological and political ways. Myths are stories, though not all stories are myths, and as *story* a myth is not simply 'a lie or a false statement to be contrasted with truth or reality or fact or history, though this usage is, perhaps, the most common meaning of myth in casual parlance today'.[6] Indeed, it is myth's capacity for ambiguity that makes it possible for it to be believed in the teeth of evidence that it is factually untrue. Take the formula with which Sudanese storytellers typically begin:

'I'm going to tell a story', they announce. 'Right!' their audience responds. 'It's a lie' they continue, 'Right!' their audience answers. 'But not everything in it is false!'[7]

Myths draw their power from groups of people that treat them as sacred stories and find their most important meaning in them. To describe the way myth functions Doniger employs the metaphor of the microscope and the telescope. Imagine a continuum of narratives that use words: at one end of the continuum is the entirely personal, e.g. a realistic novel or a diary. This end is the microscope: it is about the individual, it concerns what could or did only happen to this one person. At the other end of the continuum is the general and the abstract: this is the telescope, it is the academic treatise, the mathematical formula; it is concerned with what is true everywhere. Myth vibrates in the centre of this continuum: 'of all the things made of words' Doniger proposes, 'myths span the widest range of human concerns, human paradoxes'. Myth requires of us 'a peculiar kind of double vision' and as with physically looking through microscopic and telescopic lenses, looking through myth requires skill. It is this skill of simultaneous engagement with both ends of the narrative continuum that makes myth unique. The book of Job furnishes an example in which the microscope of Job's self-pity is whipped from his hand and replaced by God's telescope focused on the cosmos. This is the theological function of myth: to link theology with daily reality.

This wide-angle, telescopic focus in myth can also function simultaneously, Doniger maintains, as theology and as politics. Myth can realize 'the political implications of our own theological assumptions' and help to 'respect the humanity of political others by appreciating their theologies'. To be sure, some myths sound an anti-political note, by suggesting for example that there is another, higher reality more real than our own. But some myths can help us to think globally and act locally. When Otto Schindler looks down upon the liquidation of the Krakow ghetto in Spielberg's film, *Schindler's List*, in all the monochrome chaos he sees one little girl in a red coat, a single red thread through the mystery of genocide. It is this shift from the telescopic to the microscopic that bears him from indifference to compassion and from resignation to action.

Milton and Doniger hold out a lens through which to look at Bonhoeffer's interpretation of Genesis 1–3 against the political context in which he fashioned it. Of course, Milton and Bonhoeffer were not using the story of creation and Fall in the same way. Milton recast the myth with the biblical text in the background, while Bonhoeffer was offering a direct exposition of the biblical text. But the qualities of myth teased out by Doniger hold true, I think, for Bonhoeffer's exposition as much as for Milton's reworking of the same story. The political events taking place around Bonhoeffer's lecture theatre exposed fundamental questions of political life: in a setting where democracy appeared to have failed where was political authority to derive from? What is the proper nature of power and what the nature of authority? In a situation of widespread unemployment what is the place of work in human life? Events also exposed theological questions: What is the role of the Church in politics? Is political conflict an inevitable consequence of corrupt human nature?

Creation and Fall

The first sentences of *Creation and Fall* express the tension that, in Bonhoeffer's view, characterizes the relationship between the Church and the world. This tension arises from a profound difference in the orientation of the world and the Church: 'The church of Christ witnesses to the end of all things. It lives from the end, it thinks from the end, it proclaims its message from the end' (*DBW 3* 21). True, the Church lives within the old world; but its orientation to a new world spells the end for the old and 'the old world is not happy to let itself be declared dead' (*DBW 3* 21). How is it possible for the Church, which exists in time like every other institution; or the Christian, who lives like every other individual in the middle of time and history, to speak authoritatively of the beginning of the universe and of the end point of time to which the world is travelling? This human impossibility is made possible on the basis of the witness of Scripture, which knows Christ as the beginning and the end. This claim – that the Bible is the *Church's* book – proves crucial to Bonhoeffer's argument and to his exegetical method. It is the basis of his claim that these ancient Jewish texts must be read in the Church in a way that begins and ends with Jesus Christ; and it forms the presupposition of his method of 'theological exposition' of the Bible.

Bonhoeffer breaks his lectures into 22 sections, each reflecting on verses or passages in the biblical narrative. No one 'can speak of the beginning but the one who was in the beginning'. Because of this, 'God alone tells us that God is in the beginning; God testifies of God by no other means than through his word, which, as the word of a book, the words of a pious human being, is wholly a word that comes from the middle and not from the beginning' (*DBW 3* 30). The beginning described in Genesis 1 is not to be thought of in temporal terms; but as something unique, a limit beyond which human beings cannot go. The character of this beginning, Bonhoeffer asserts, can only be known in the resurrection, which is, like God's creation, a creating out of nothing.

In other ancient creation myths a deity creates by imparting something of its own nature to creation. But in the Bible, God's being is never mixed in with what God creates. There is, then, nothing that unites God with creation except God's *word* (*DBW 3* 40). God is not bound to creation, God does not enter creation, but is in the world 'only' in the word. With Martin Luther, Bonhoeffer distinguished God's role as Creator from God's role as *preserver* of creation. This was to counter two erroneous understandings, as he saw them, of God's relation to what God creates. During the Enlightenment the Deists proposed that God was the Prime Mover, the first cause, who created the world but then passively sat back as creation carried on with no further divine involvement. A second view, increasingly prevalent in Germany among pro-Nazi theologians, was that God not only created the world but constantly intervenes within it in new acts of creation, for example bringing about the German *Volk*. Bonhoeffer maintained that God not only created the world, but is involved daily with it to preserve what God created. Yet speaking of that involvement as 'creation' risks implying that there was something imperfect in the original creation that God must tinker with until God gets it right. God does not continually wrest creation out of nothingness, but upholds and affirms creation in itself, even though it is fallen.

In the opening verses of Genesis 1 that which God creates is dead. Only in verse 11 does God create something living from something dead, not by a process of evolution, but by divine command. Yet that which lives does not run of its own accord for if God withdraws from his work the world sinks back into nothingness. The creation of life to this point in the narrative was good, but still God did not recognize God's self in what had been made. Only with the creation of human beings does God create something that resembles the Creator? The creation of humanity differs from the creation of other living things in several ways. God does not simply call humankind forth out of non-being, as was the case with all God's previous creative acts; humankind is taken up into God's planning. Human beings are certainly connected with the animals, but their peculiar relation to God, which is expressed in terms of image and likeness, distinguishes them alone. This relationship is not to be thought of as a likeness of *being*, an *analogia entis*, but rather, as an *analogia relationis*. 'What this means', Bonhoeffer explains, 'is firstly, that the *relatio* [the relationship] too is not a human potential or possibility or a structure of human existence; instead it is a given relationship, a relation in which human beings are set, a *justitia passiva*! [passive righteousness]' (*DBW 3* 65). It is a likeness derived entirely from the one who is the prototype to whom the likeness points, and is not a quality of human being independent from its source. The Sabbath marks the blessing and completion of the first creation narrative.

If the first creation narrative is for Bonhoeffer about humankind for God thought out from above; then the second is about God for humankind, thought out from below. The two narratives therefore complement rather than contradict one another. The anthropomorphisms of the Yahwist account of the creation of Adam (in Genesis 1–2:4a) are, Bonhoeffer acknowledges, insupportably childlike. However, he brushes this off because 'in being distinguished as the word of God it [the story] is quite simply the *source* of knowledge about the origin of humankind' (*DBW 3* 75–6). It expresses the physical nearness of the Creator to the creature, but also God's omnipotence. This is the background to a remark Bonhoeffer now makes that echoes Wendy Doniger's account of the nature and value of myth. 'Who can speak of these things', he asks, 'except in pictures? Pictures after all are not lies; rather they indicate things and enable the underlying meaning to shine through' (*DBW 3* 81). The exposition that follows must therefore 'seek to translate the old picture language of the magical world into the new picture language of the technical world' (*DBW 3* 83).

In the centre of Eden stand two trees: the tree of knowledge of good and evil, and the tree of life. Bonhoeffer mentions historical critical analysis of the two trees, but only to dismiss it by reiterating that 'our concern is the text as it presents itself to the church today'. The tree of life is at the centre as God is at the centre of Adam's life in the Garden. 'The distinctive characteristic of Adam's life is utterly unbroken and unified obedience, that is, Adam's innocence and ignorance of disobedience' (*DBW 3* 84). Adam understands the limit imposed by God's word. It is not because he can distinguish between good and evil that Adam understands his limit. Rather, the prohibition to eat the fruit of the tree indicated on the one hand his freedom, and on the other the limit of his human creatureliness. This boundary or limit to the human condition is not at the limit of his capacities, as if it marked the limits of human technology or ingenuity or capability: it is a limit at the centre of human life. The limit is God, and the limit is grace.

Adam's loneliness is an anticipation of the loneliness of human life. Christ is alone because he alone loves the other person; we are alone, because we have hated others and pushed them away. Eve is created by God as Adam's partner to share his limits and his life. At the beginning of chapter 3, after the creation of the first human community of husband and wife, Bonhoeffer titles his next section 'the pious question'. The serpent is not, for Bonhoeffer, an incarnation of the devil, but one of God's creatures who becomes an instrument of evil. By spelling this out Bonhoeffer sidesteps the question of how evil came into the world, justifying the evasion on the basis that the biblical narrative of the Fall does not address the question either. The serpent is subtle: to begin with he does not dispute God's word. His question, 'Did God really say?' is apparently innocent. Bonhoeffer describes his exchange with Eve as the first religious conversation and the first theological debate. But the question opens up a brave new world of possibilities unsuspected by Eve in her innocence. 'The decisive point', Bonhoeffer explains,

> is that through this question the idea is suggested to the human being of going behind the word of God and now providing it with a human basis – a human understanding of the essential nature of God. Should the word contradict this understanding, then the human being has clearly misheard. (*DBW* 3 106)

So what, Bonhoeffer continues, 'is the real evil in this question?':

> It is not that a question as such is asked. It is that this question already contains the wrong answer. It is that with this question the basic attitude of the creature toward the Creator comes under attack. It requires humankind to sit in judgement on God's word instead of simply listening to it and doing it. And this is achieved by proposing that, on the basis of an idea, a principle, or some prior knowledge about God, humankind should now pass judgement on the concrete word of God. (*DBW 3* 107–8)

When Eve still resists temptation, the serpent takes a more aggressive line, suggesting to her that God's prohibition of the tree's fruit is intended to prevent Eve and Adam becoming '*sicut deus*', like God: eat of the fruit, lies the serpent, and you too can be like God. Eating the fruit removes a limit, as the serpent suggested it would, and makes Eve and Adam *sicut deus*, at the centre, but alone. Humankind 'now lives out of its own resources, creates its own life, is its own creator; it no longer needs the Creator, it has itself become the creator, inasmuch as it creates its own life' (*DBW 3* 115).

After the Fall, already before their expulsion from the garden, Eve and Adam experience shame. To Bonhoeffer, shame and conscience are symptoms of the fallen state of humanity. Shame, he asserts, is 'an unwilling pointer to revelation, to the limit, to the other, to God' (*DBW 3* 124). It points to revelation because it draws attention to the fallen nature of humankind, but, since it is a result of that fallen nature, it is *not* itself something good – a common, flawed, 'moralistic, puritanical' interpretation. The word God addresses to Eve and Adam as they flee God is a word of both curse and of promise. It is *curse* as God's affirmation that paradise is destroyed and that humanity must now live out of its own resources, *sicut deus*. It is *promise* in that, even though it is a word of anger and judgement, it is God's word, and accompanies humanity in its new life. Work falls under the same curse, as it fastens humanity's separateness from nature in toil. At the same time it is promise, in that human beings are permitted to go on living alongside the natural world from which they have separated themselves. Bonhoeffer's account concludes by reiterating that 'the creator is now the preserver; the created world is now the fallen *but preserved world*' (*DBW 3* 139). The final verse of chapter 3, announcing Cain's birth, is for Bonhoeffer intrinsic to the story of the Fall as it marks the beginning of human community in the fallen world.

What was new in Bonhoeffer's Genesis lectures?

Though it is sensible not to set too much store by student recollections gathered years after the events they describe, they may help us to gain an impression of the freshness of Bonhoeffer's theology for students in the early 1930s. One Berlin student recalled being struck by Bonhoeffer's way of turning things round, 'away from where they were stored for everyday use, to the place God had ordained for them ... in the process the values that had been so familiar and natural to us were transformed as if by themselves'.[8] Another found his exegesis hard to take, and thought the lectures were 'fairy tales' lacking in philosophical rigour (*DBW 3* 3). Similar reactions were provoked when on 10 October 1934 Bonhoeffer gave a talk at Richmond Methodist College in London. Bonhoeffer spoke on the situation in Germany by using again his insights on creation and Fall. One member of his audience remembered 'that he seemed to take the Genesis stories as factual history whereas we were all obsessed with the theory of evolution! We were in a different thought world. My impression was that he convinced no one because we were working from different premises.'[9] Bonhoeffer's hermeneutic perturbed another Richmond student for whom this was his first encounter with Barthianism: 'I recall feeling "here is a man who respects every word of Scripture, but he treats Scripture in an allegorical way, a sort of Alexandrine *redivivus*"'.[10] These remarks underline the extent to which Bonhoeffer's theological exposition of the Old Testament jarred with prevailing patterns of biblical exegesis in Germany and in England. Dogmatic theology rarely engaged in biblical exegesis, and biblical exegesis was in thrall to the methods of historical criticism.

So what was new in Bonhoeffer's theology? John de Gruchy (*DBW 3* 5–12) discerns five ways in which the lectures constitute a turning point in Bonhoeffer's theological development. Firstly Bonhoeffer's method of *theological exposition of scripture* marked a new turn. *Creation and Fall* was 'Bonhoeffer's first attempt to do theology in direct dialogue with the Bible' (*DBW 3* 6). Karl Barth's commentary on Paul's letter to the Romans might have created controversy, but theologians all took Paul's theology seriously. The Genesis myths on the other hand, outside the guild of Old Testament scholarship, were widely regarded as primitive legends with little relevance to modern life. Biblical scholars characterized their discipline as *scientific*; a critical and therefore objective commentary on the biblical text. Few thought it part of their job to interpret the Bible theologically for contemporary ecclesial or even political life. Bonhoeffer tried not to dismiss scholarly insights altogether, but his concern was with the word of God for the Church, and for the witness of the Church to the world.

A second way, de Gruchy continues, in which Bonhoeffer's theological development pivots on these lectures was in his distinctive use of the Old Testament. In *Creation and Fall* Bonhoeffer read the Bible as a book of the Church, believing that 'it *is* this in its very essence, or it is nothing' (*DBW 3* 22). The third way in which the lectures signal something new follows on from this insight; not only did Bonhoeffer believe that the Bible must be read as a book of the Church, he believed that the whole of the Bible should be read within the Church as a book of Christ. The uncompromising Christocentrism of Bonhoeffer's reading of the Hebrew Bible, in the wake of the Holocaust, creates obvious theological problems; but this should not obfuscate the originality of Bonhoeffer's commitment to recovering the Old Testament for Christian theology in a climate in which it was widely dismissed as irrelevant.

Creation and Fall is, fourthly, a turning point in its emphasis on human freedom in relation to the *freedom of God*. For Bonhoeffer, God gives human beings freedom to rule responsibly over creation. This means that human freedom is freedom 'for others'. Finally, the lectures are a turning point in opening up a *theology of nature*. As a Lutheran, Bonhoeffer was concerned with the trend in Lutheran theology, to view the German nation as a divinely instituted 'order of creation'. Bonhoeffer took from Luther a distinction between God's creative act and God's ongoing role in preserving or sustaining what God has created. On this basis Bonhoeffer coins the term 'orders of preservation'. In his ethics, he would return to this theme, recasting the 'orders of preservation' as the 'divine mandates'. With both terms Bonhoeffer attempts to redress an abandonment of the natural order by Protestant theology. Bonhoeffer's theology here foreshadows Stanley Hauerwas's recent insistence that a theology rooted in the witness of Scripture to the incarnation of Jesus Christ is in conflict with a theology of the natural, properly understood, but works, in John H. Yoder's captivating phrase 'with the grain of the universe'.

Two questions revisited

The Fall, theology and politics

I want now to take up the two lines of questions with which I began this chapter and to suggest two ways, further to those suggested by de Gruchy, in which the lectures constitute a turning point in Bonhoeffer's career.

Bonhoeffer's lectures on *Creation and Fall* are a turning point, I suggest, in Bonhoeffer's theological *engagement with the political*. Bonhoeffer had a longstanding interest in politics, but it was while he was lecturing on Genesis that he first makes an explicit attempt to comment publicly on political matters. It was not simply that he now had something particular to comment on, but that something about his reading of Genesis opened up a connection between theology and politics that had previously been closed. On 1 February 1933, two days after the Berlin crowds had enthusiastically acclaimed Hitler's appointment as Reich Chancellor, Bonhoeffer gave a radio broadcast on 'The Younger Generation's Altered View of the Concept of the Führer', a topic he had chosen before Hitler assumed power. The politically controversial nature of the address may be the reason it was cut off before Bonhoeffer had finished speaking. Bonhoeffer gave a longer reflection on the same theme in a lecture at Berlin's Technische Hochschule. The addresses are both theological *and* political. Bonhoeffer breaks down the 'younger generation' into groups who depend for their views on the experiences of their age group: the oldest is the generation of war veterans; the youngest, those not affected directly by the experience of war, and who live in the shadow of their elders. The war marked the bitter triumph of technology and machines and the failure of political ideologies. It released the dull power of the masses in politics and emphasized the insignificance of the individual. Above all, this effected a sea change in German attitudes towards power and authority. Before the war, authority figures in Germany derived their authority from the office they held; as teachers, as lawyers, as Pastors, or parents or as politicians. And because their authority was that of an office holder, those in authority accepted that their authority had boundaries and limits. The Führer, Bonhoeffer argues, does not derive his authority from an office, but from the loyalty of those who follow him. This has two dangerous consequences: it makes his authority limitless, in contrast with that of the office holder, and paradoxically it makes him dependent on the whim of those who follow him. It was not the loss of democracy that troubled Bonhoeffer in the collapse of the Weimar constitution, but the loss of the law, the loss of the limits that constrain office holders in the exercise of their authority. This characterization of German politics very nearly implies that a political Fall had taken place during the period of the Weimar constitution. In the earlier political era of Empire Bonhoeffer implies that office holders accepted the limits of their office as Adam accepted the limitation of God's command not to eat of the tree of knowledge, while *after the Fall* of the Weimar constitution the Führer arrogated to himself the *sicut deus* of power without the boundary of law. Bonhoeffer's anxiety is that the Führer is becoming for the younger generation a verführer, the leader a misleader. The Führer is the serpent, tempting the young to make themselves like God.[11]

The connection between Bonhoeffer's political awakening and his exegesis of Genesis 1–3 is made explicit in the talk he gave at Richmond Methodist College in October 1934. The only contemporary record of Bonhoeffer's address on this occasion is a journal entry by John Wright, who hosted Bonhoeffer for the evening. Wright recorded that Bonhoeffer spoke on the situation in Germany by exploring the issue of authority. Authority, Bonhoeffer argued, takes three forms. *Logical authority* 'wrecks itself on human wisdom' since the incarnation contradicts reason and logic. Under the heading '*psychological authority*' Bonhoeffer contrasted experience and faith: the German Christians claimed a new revelation in National Socialism. But faith, Bonhoeffer asserted, 'can only exist where there is no experience'; it is 'trust in defiance of reason'. In Paradise, therefore, there was no scope for the reasoning of conscience, since conscience assumes knowledge of good and evil that Adam did not have before his expulsion from the Garden. *Historical authority* assumes that there is a part of the world that is *not* fallen, such as the Church, or an infallible Bible. But the only part of the world that is free from sin, the only ultimate authority, is Jesus Christ. This is the political explication of the Christocentric hermeneutics of *Creation and Fall* that pulls the rug of authority from beneath the feet of the Nazis and the German Christians.

The distinctiveness of Christian ethics

Bonhoeffer's use of the Genesis myths provides a link to one further way in which *Creation and Fall* marks a significant turning point: by means of this myth Bonhoeffer distinguishes Christian ethics from all other ethics. 'The knowledge of good and evil seems to be the aim of all ethical reflection', Bonhoeffer would write in his *Ethics*, 'The first task of Christian ethics is to invalidate this knowledge'. In this way 'Christian ethics claims to discuss the origin of the whole problem of ethics, and thus professes to be a critique of all ethics simply as ethics' (*E* 3). Thus, in his full ethical maturity, Bonhoeffer would repeat the insight developed in *Creation and Fall* that 'humanity at its origin knows only one thing: God', and thus 'the knowledge of good and evil shows that he is no longer at one with this origin'. The knowledge of good and evil is not, therefore, knowledge of the good and evil of God, but of good and evil against God. Jesus alone lives not by the knowledge of good and evil but by the will of God. It is Christ who opens the possibility of a world of recovered unity, but only for those who are prepared to move, using Nietzsche's phrase, 'beyond good and evil' in simple obedience to God.

Bonhoeffer's claim that Christian ethics is distinct from all other ethics is every bit as emphatic as Stanley Hauerwas's and it raises similar questions. It was easier for John Milton: when he wrote of the Fall he was using a story that was used in the Church and in the extra-ecclesial world of politics, and worked differently but effectively in both spheres. For Bonhoeffer – as for us – connecting theology and politics makes different demands because the Bible is no longer both a 'book of the Church' and a source for public ethics so that the links between Christian ethics and other ethics are no longer obvious. So how we express the relationship of the Church and the (secular) world makes a deal of difference. From the Church's point of view, Bonhoeffer and Hauerwas insist, Christian ethics is at one with God. And in obedience to God Christians are at one with the natural, working with the grain of the universe. It is all other ethics that are fissiparous, all other ethics that are dualistic, all other ethics that are sectarian; for by claiming the knowledge of good and evil they live in the wake of the divisive sin of Eve and Adam. But does this insight – that Christian ethics is distinct from all other ethics – really enable political action, as Bonhoeffer believed, or does it separate Christian ethics and public ethics in such a way as to permit no dialogue between them? Something of an answer lies in the idea of divine limits to secular authority and of the relation of human freedom to the freedom of God. If Hauerwas is right it shouldn't matter that Bonhoeffer failed to prevent the Confessing Church turning in on itself, or that the conspiracy failed to remove Hitler: he was a faithful witness, and that is all that matters. Success, Bonhoeffer wrote, is a temptation. But it is hard to evade the feeling that if the world can simply go about its business without paying any attention to the witness of Christian politics and ethics, whatever its quality before God, something is still not quite right. *Creation and Fall* set the parameters of Bonhoeffer's ethical enquiry: what he needed now was to delineate its content.

Notes

1   *With the Grain of the Universe*, Stanley Hauerwas, SCM, 2002.

2   *Milton and the English Revolution*, Christopher Hill, Faber & Faber, 1977, p. 344.

3   Ibid., p. 345.

4   Ibid., p. 344.

5   *The Implied Spider*, Wendy Doniger, Columbia University Press, 1998.

6   Ibid., p. 2.

7   Ibid.

8   Wolf Dieter Zimmerman in *I knew Dietrich Bonhoeffer*, ed. Wolf Dieter Zimmerman and Ronald Gregor Smith, Fontana, 1973.

9   Percy Scott, personal communication, 15 March 1989, in 'Uses of the Bible in the Ethics of Dietrich Bonhoeffer', Stephen Plant, Cambridge University PhD, 1993.

10   Reginald Kissack, personal communication, 18 March 1989, ibid.

11   Bonhoeffer's political views, which included antipathy, for Germany, towards a liberal democratic political system, and sympathy for some form of legal oligarchy, are uncomfortable for those formed by the assumptions of liberal democracy. Among Bonhoeffer scholars the issue is generally avoided.

6

Following Christ

The call of Saint Matthew

Genius does not always keep company with gentility. Michelangelo Merisi da Caravaggio (1573–1610) was the finest Italian painter of the seventeenth century, equally brilliant in executing epic subjects and domestic life.[1] He was also a man with an evil temper. At the height of his career, when in spite of a poor personal reputation he was attracting the most prestigious commissions in Rome, he killed a man in a brawl and fled the Papal city in fear of arrest. Four years later his artistic skill won him a pardon, but a series of misadventures befell him on his journey to Rome and he died, isolated and desperate, success draining through his fingers like water through the hands of a thirsty man. Caravaggio gained his artistic reputation painting scenes from the Roman backstreets in which he was at home. He painted musicians and gypsies, cardsharps, glistening fruit, violent scenes and pretty boys; he celebrated courtly graces and damned the cost. He lit his paintings as if they were stage sets;[2] he painted the bubbles in a glass of red wine and the bloom of an apple with sublime veracity. But his use of artistic models from Rome's seamy side gave a subversive edge to his work. Even the patrons who could afford a Caravaggio were not at all certain they wanted to be reminded of the faces the other side of their palazzo walls.

Caravaggio was therefore a risky choice to paint three works for the Saint Matthew side chapel of San Luigi dei Francesi. Not only was he unknown as a painter of religious subjects, it was very likely he would use the vagabonds, rakes and whores with whom he kept company as models for his holy subjects. When he came to Matthew's call, Caravaggio boldly set his painting in a Roman back street. As some had feared, he used his friends as his models. The boy in a feathered hat who leans casually on the Saint's shoulder had last appeared in Caravaggio's painting of a youth conned by a fortune-teller, and while others in the work are unidentifiable their freshness suggests they were painted from life. To the left of the painting Matthew and four companions sit beside a table more evocative of card playing than counting taxes. One youth carries a sword; another is lost in contemplation of the coins that lie on the table. An old man wears spectacles, the better to see the money that occupies his gaze. The men around the table are dressed in fine clothes – fur-lined collars and feathered hats. They wear striking colours: gold and red, black and white, blue and red in silk and velvet. In every way in contrast to the scene at the table, to the right of the picture stand two men in drab and simple clothes, Jesus and Peter. Jesus' arm stretches towards Matthew and his hand, in a gesture borrowed from the hand of Adam in the Sistine Chapel, points towards Matthew who, astonished, points at himself to ask if it really is him whom Jesus calls. The room in which the drama takes place is as shady as the characters in it, but a shaft of light follows the line of Jesus' hand and illuminates Matthew's face.

Yet the most astonishing feature of Caravaggio's painting is that while Jesus and Peter wear simple togas – as the artist imagined they would in the first century Levant – the men around the table wear clothes contemporary with the time and place of the painting: Rome at the turn of the seventeenth century. The painting holds together two periods of time, the past and the present, and links them solely by the power of Jesus' call. The effect is to lift the call of Matthew from the antique world of the first century into the immediacy of the present. It refocuses attention from Jesus calling Matthew to the call he makes now to whoever sees the painting with faithful eyes. By means of the lived-in faces of the friends who modelled for him and by conveying a sense of the living interrelationship of the past and the present, Caravaggio bridges the hermeneutical gap between Jesus' call to Matthew and his call to us, between Scripture and its readers.

There is no evidence that Bonhoeffer ever saw Caravaggio's depiction of Matthew's call; in the diary he kept of his stay in Rome he seems to have favoured Rome's classical to its Renaissance aspect. In any case it is a pity he did not know it better: Caravaggio's 'The calling of St Matthew' is the perfect frontispiece and illustration for Bonhoeffer's theology of discipleship. Like the painting, Bonhoeffer's theology is dominated by the presence of Christ. In both *The calling of St Matthew* and *Discipleship*, Scripture is lifted with shocking effect into the present, and in both the effect is to refocus attention away from historical study towards Jesus' call to me, here and now. *Discipleship* is Bonhoeffer's longest book and *Life Together* probably his most widely read. Like Caravaggio's painting, these books created controversy when published because they attempted to make real a sense of what Jesus wants from us today. They are rich sources for Christian ethics. It will be the task of this chapter to give an idea of what his contemporaries found so shocking in these books and to ask in what ways Bonhoeffer's theology in them raises ethical questions or offers ethical insight.

Christology

In 1933, in the semester following his lectures on *Creation and Fall*, Bonhoeffer's theology took a turn to Jesus Christ from which it would not thereafter deviate. In his lectures on christology, Bonhoeffer realized both the centrality of Christ in theology and of the person of Christ within the Christian life. Attending to them at this point rather than in the previous chapter may seem arbitrary: there are three years between the christology lectures and the publication of *Discipleship*. But the gestation period of Bonhoeffer's *Discipleship* was long and he was already drafting sections of the book when he took up his London pastorate in 1933. Reading the christology lectures at this point in any case helps to show how Bonhoeffer's discovery of Jesus Christ in 1933 was prerequisite to his theology of discipleship and the common life. The manuscript of Bonhoeffer's lectures no longer exists and they have been reconstructed on the basis of notes taken by several students. The third section of the lectures – the Eternal Christ – was never delivered.

Bonhoeffer's opening gambit is as simple as it is arresting: in so far as the Church speaks of Christ, he says, it does so first in silence before the mystery of God's word. To most people, the study of Christ may seem an academic backwater, but for Bonhoeffer christology is *the* academic discipline which makes all others possible. Scientific study, by which he means not only the natural sciences but humanities disciplines too, asks two basic questions: 'what is the cause of X?' and 'what is the meaning of X?' By means of these 'how' questions the human mind seeks to make sense of the world by cataloguing and classifying all the knowledge it gathers. But what happens when a Word (in Greek, 'logos') appears that cannot be classified by the human mind, but rather puts the human logos in its place by making it the subject of enquiry. Then, the important question is not the 'how' of the human being, but the question 'who?' Who are you to challenge me in this way? Are you God? Only when christology resists the temptation to ask how questions about Christ – for example 'how is Christ both God and man?' – and instead lies open to the question 'who is Jesus Christ for us today?' does it become truly authentic. In christology, reflection upon the person of Christ always precedes reflection upon what he does, since our understanding of Christ's person makes every difference to our understanding of his works.

In the first part of the lectures, Bonhoeffer explores the senses in which Christ is present *'pro me'* – for me in the world. As the crucified and risen one, Christ's presence is realized in space and time. Picking up where *Sanctorum Communio* left off, Bonhoeffer reiterates that Christ is present in the Church. So significant is this, that where Christ is not present in preaching and sacrament, christology is impossible. It is not simply that Christ's influence persists in the Church as a memory; he is present as a living person. Human logic finds what is involved in this truth hard to accommodate, for as a man, Christ is present in time and space, and as God he is eternally present. Because he is always both a human being and God – Bonhoeffer uses the term God-Man – we cannot treat the question of his presence as *either* his presence as a man *or* his presence as God, but only by talking about his whole person. There is simply no point asking – as Kierkegaard does – how God the eternal can be present in time, or asking how the historical Jesus can be present now, 2000 years after his death. We can only ask how the God-Man Jesus Christ is present. Because of this, Christ's presence for me is hidden. It is not that God is hidden in a human being but rather that as a whole person the God-Man is hidden in 'the likeness of sinful flesh' (Romans 8:3). Bonhoeffer refutes here a very common interpretation of the incarnation: that the 'scandal' of Christ lay in God taking human flesh. Rather, the offence of Jesus is that he took *sinful* flesh; that is his humiliation.

For Bonhoeffer, Christ's presence takes three forms. As Word, Christ takes the living form of God's address to human beings. As such, he is not an idea, a new truth or a new moral teaching, but God's appeal to each human person to assume responsibility. Jesus does not merely speak this word of address; he is the Word. In this sense the Word is made available in the preaching. This is why the sermon is not properly conceived as words spoken by a preacher, but as the Word of God. Christ is present, too, in the sacraments, which are not only representations of Christ, but in a literal sense, *embodiments* of the Word. The Church is not a symbol of Christ's body, but is his body in the world. Christ as Word, sacrament and Church is therefore at the centre of human existence.

Christ is at the centre of human existence as the judgement and justification that all people must face. When it comes to speaking of Christ as the centre of history, Bonhoeffer cautions against trying to prove that Christianity is somehow the highpoint of human religions, or arguing that Christ is central because the Church plays a central role in the life of a nation. Christ is the centre of history because he mediates between God and humankind, and between God and history. Finally, Christ stands at the centre between God and nature. Nature was cursed at the Fall, but it is redeemed by Jesus Christ who stands between God and nature to bring about their reconciliation.

In the second part of his christology lectures Bonhoeffer tackles the question of 'the historical Christ'. A typical manoeuvre in nineteenth and twentieth-century christology was to distinguish between the historical person of Jesus of Nazareth, and the Christ of faith. This method – which von Harnack and others promised would release the core of faith from its unnecessary outer coating – was from Bonhoeffer's point of view mistaken both historically and theologically. Historically, all attempts to discover a 'pure' early life of Jesus in the gospels had failed conspicuously. Theologically, one cannot get behind belief in the Lordship of Christ. Because of this failure, Bonhoeffer asserted bravely in his lecture hall in the heartland of liberal theology, liberal theology could no longer sustain the difference between Jesus and Christ and the Bible could only be interpreted in the Church, where Christ's Lordship is presupposed.

As it was commonly taught, the study of christology examined the development of the orthodox christological statements of the creeds and subsequently, for Protestants, in the founding documents of Lutherans and Calvinists. The creeds are official statements of the Church. A creative, positive christology goes on, of course, all the time in sermon, liturgy, doxology and theology. But this positive christology has to be subjected to rigorous criticism. In this sense the creeds are negative statements placing limits on what may be said of Christ. Bonhoeffer diligently takes his students through the christological heresies of the early Church, and the founding statements of the Protestant churches. These set of boundaries against false interpretations of the person of Christ. He concludes that while no true theology of Christ can transgress the boundaries set by these negative christologies, neither can christology be satisfied with them. In the final sections of the extant lectures, Bonhoeffer deals with the incarnation of Christ, and with his humiliation and exaltation, in which he hints at themes developed more fully in his later theology. Significantly, these include an emphasis on the weakness of Christ. If we are really to speak of Christ's divinity, we may not look first at Jesus' human nature and then beyond it, to his divine nature: we must only ever look at the one man, Jesus Christ who is fully human and fully God. As a result, it is impossible to identify Jesus' weakness with his humanity by saying 'as a man Jesus was weak, but as God he was strong'. It is the whole God-Man who is weak. This insight would crop up again with decisive effect in Bonhoeffer's prison letters. In a less obvious way, as Eberhard Bethge points out, christology 'was to be the basis for ethics and the refutation of the "orders of creation" concept' (*DB* 219). For now, the centrality of Christ spelled out in the lectures paved the way for what would prove to be the longest writing project of Bonhoeffer's career: *Discipleship*.

Following Jesus

Shortly after *Discipleship* was published Bonhoeffer wrote to the students he had trained at Zingst and Finkenwalde to let them know it was out. 'When it appeared', he wrote:

> I dedicated it in spirit to you all. I would have done so on the title page had I not feared to lay the responsibility for my theology and my ideas on your shoulders … In any case you all know what's in it. (*DB* 452)

Yes, they knew. The bulk of the book was made up of the lectures Bonhoeffer had given to students in the Confessing Church Seminary he directed. Bonhoeffer's seminary students were not dissimilar to those entering Ministerial training today: they came expecting to brush up their techniques, learn some of the practicalities of Ministry, and practise leading worship. But *Discipleship* shattered these expectations by knocking down their presuppositions of preaching, sacramental and pastoral ministry, and seeking to rebuild them on new foundations. The book falls into two parts. The first part largely takes the form of exegesis of passages from the Synoptic gospels. Part two turns to the Church and, though often referring to the Epistles, takes the form of 'Bible study' rather less. In *Discipleship,* Bonhoeffer writes with a new confidence. It is as if he has found his own voice. The book retains some of the qualities of the lectures – rhetorical flourishes, some phrases repeated for emphasis, others with the memorability and force of sound bites – that keep the reader in touch with the book's key themes. Yet *Discipleship* has a disturbing style that draws one into its vocabulary and perspective to the point that one forgets all other modulations in and forms of theology. This siren-like quality is the book's strength and its weakness. In the flow of the book's language and approach one feels there can be no other way of understanding Christian faith; but re-enter a context in which faith is foreign and it can be hard to make the book connect.

At about the same time as Bonhoeffer was writing *Discipleship,* his erstwhile ethics teacher, Reinhold Niebuhr, was arguing in *An interpretation of Christian Ethics*[3] that New Testament ethical teaching, whether of Jesus or of Paul, was given in anticipation of an imminent second coming which did not, in fact, materialize. For Niebuhr this meant that the ethics of Jesus and Paul were only ever intended for a brief interim period and were therefore unsustainable, taken literally, as a basis of modern Christian morality. Bonhoeffer could scarcely have disagreed more with his former teacher. He believed that the Church Struggle drew out more searching ways of reading Scripture from readers who do not seek to know what this or that church leader wants, but rather, 'want to know what Jesus wants' (*DBW 4*: 37). Bonhoeffer begins therefore with an assault on cheap grace:

> Cheap grace is the mortal enemy of our church. Our struggle today is for costly grace.
> Cheap grace means grace as bargain-basement goods, cut-rate forgiveness, cut-rate comfort, cut-rate sacrament; grace as the church's inexhaustible pantry, from which it is doled out by careless hands without hesitation or limit. It is grace without a price, without costs. (*DBW 4* 43)

Cheap grace means justification of sin but not of the sinner. It is:

[P]reaching forgiveness without repentance; it is baptism without the discipline of community; it is the Lord's Supper without confession of sin; it is absolution without personal confession. Cheap grace is grace without discipleship, grace without the cross, grace without the living, incarnate Jesus Christ. (*DBW 4* 44)

In contrast, costly grace is the gospel that costs everything. It is costly because it condemns sin and grace, because it justifies the sinner. Above all, grace is costly because God paid its price in the incarnation and the crucifixion. Original awareness of the cost of grace within the Church, Bonhoeffer alleges, seeped away as the world was Christianized and the Church secularized. Luther reawakened a true sense of the cost of grace in the Reformation, but this too has been lost: 'A people became Christian, became Lutheran, but at the cost of discipleship, at an all-too-cheap price' (*DBW 4* 53). In preaching to an entire nation, baptizing, confirming and absolving a people unconditionally, Bonhoeffer glumly concludes, Lutherans poured out rivers of grace without end but only rarely accompanied this with the call rigorously to follow Christ.

To explain what the call to discipleship is like Bonhoeffer turns to the call of Matthew. When Jesus called the tax collector he did not respond with a confession of faith, but by getting up from his table and following Jesus. Bonhoeffer can see that there is something unreasonable in Matthew's response; the sensible thing to do would have been to think about his decision, weigh the consequences, and think before acting. He simply obeys. Strikingly, discipleship has no content other than following Jesus. No 'new law' is involved, no programme for life: just unreserved commitment to Christ. It is not a call for which one can 'volunteer', because the call must come from Jesus. Nothing, not even religious duty, must be allowed to come between Jesus and the disciple. Neither is following Jesus something to be lifted off a shelf of life-choices, as if Christian faith were one human way of life among others. The call of Jesus to the disciple is unique and decisive. This is Jesus' role in calling the disciple, but the disciple too has something to contribute. For Bonhoeffer as a Lutheran theologian, suggesting that the disciple might make a contribution to faith was hedged about with problems. Luther's rediscovery of costly grace involved a thorough rejection of faith by works – the idea that a believer could contribute to her own salvation by what she did, for example by good deeds or acts of penance. Lutheranism held up its hands in horror at any suggestion that discipleship was based on anything other than Jesus' call. Bonhoeffer accepts this insofar as he agrees that the situation where faith is possible is only made possible by Christ's call, and can only come about by faith. Yet he maintains that the potential disciple must herself take a step towards Jesus, rather as Peter did when he left the boat and walked on water at Jesus' invitation (Matthew 14:29). The formula Bonhoeffer uses to express the balance between faith and the step a would-be disciple takes towards it is *'only the believers obey,* and *only the obedient believe' (DBW 4* 63). It is not the case, Bonhoeffer believes, that first there is faith, and then there is obedience, or, indeed, that first there is obedience and then there is faith, in some invariable chronological sequence. The two sides of this equation must always be held together. To make this clearer, Bonhoeffer uses the example of the rich young ruler who asked Jesus, 'Teacher, what good deed must I do to have eternal life?' (Matthew 19:16–22).[4] The ruler addresses his question to Jesus as 'good master', but Jesus refuses the title since only God is good. This serves to make clear, Bonhoeffer says, that when Jesus calls, the call is not from some human teacher or guru, but from God. When Jesus tells him to obey the commandments, the young man 'retreats from God's clear commandment back to the interesting, indisputably human situation of "ethical conflict"' (*DBW 4* 71) by asking 'which ones?' as if God's commandments were unclear. Consistent with the views he had expressed in *Creation and Fall*, Bonhoeffer asserts that to 'invoke ethical conflict is to terminate obedience. It is to retreat from God's reality to human possibility, from faith to doubt' (*DBW 4* 71). Jesus refuses to resolve this ethical conflict, and answers it in the only way God can: by making a direct command to the young man. Sadly, the ruler leaves, for he cannot easily give up his riches as directed.

How does the call to simple obedience made by Jesus to Matthew, and Peter, and the rich young ruler relate to us? Does Jesus call us in the same way, and must our response take the same form? When a modern reader reads Jesus' command to the rich young ruler to sell all he has and give to the poor, he will find ways of not taking this literally. He will think 'the command was made to a specific individual, he cannot possibly mean that I should do the same'; or 'what Jesus really means is that I should not set my heart on possessions, so if I can sit lightly to material wealth then I don't need literally to sell what I own and give it away'. For Bonhoeffer, such strategies can add up to a 'deliberate avoidance of simple, literal obedience' (*DBW 4* 79). To be sure, it is right for Christians to read the Bible with discernment and to have what Bonhoeffer calls (after Kierkegaard) a 'paradoxical understanding of the commandment'; but it is 'necessary always to include a literal understanding of Jesus' commandment in every paradoxical interpretation'. This means that at the heart of our justifiably sophisticated ways of reading Jesus' words, Christians must not lose sight of the possibility that Jesus speaks to us to command simple obedience within the pages of the Bible. Such obedience, Bonhoeffer reiterates, is costly, as it will mean not only suffering with Christ but also more painfully sharing in his rejection.

Jesus' ethic is, for Bonhoeffer, at its most clear and most startling in the Sermon on the Mount. In the Beatitudes Jesus addresses his followers and with each word of 'blessing' he spells out the differences between the disciple and the unbeliever. Disciples are blessed in their poverty, where it is assumed for the sake of Christ: in this respect Jesus' blessing is the opposite of 'its caricature in the form of a political-social program' (*DBW 4* 103), that is, 'blessing' cannot be equated with the alleviation of material poverty. They are blessed in their grief – not as Bonhoeffer understands it their normal human grief for a lost loved one – but in their grief over the guilt and fate of the world. The meek are blessed as those who 'renounce all rights of their own for the sake of Jesus Christ' (*DBW 4* 105). They endure violence and abuse without answering back because they leave justice to God, for whose righteousness alone they thirst. In giving mercy, the disciples are blessed as women and men who renounce their own dignity by sharing in the guilt and need of others. They are pure in heart because, in their simple obedience, they have 'the simple heart of a child, who does not know about good and evil, the heart of Adam before the fall, the heart in which the will of Jesus rules instead of one's own conscience' (*DBW 4* 107). 'Simple obedience' is clearly here the link between Bonhoeffer's early exposition of Genesis 3, and reflection on the world of 'recovered unity' in his *Ethics*. The disciples are blessed also in their renunciation of violence and strife – the scriptural warrant for Bonhoeffer's pacifism – and in being prepared to be persecuted for the sake of a righteous cause. Where Jesus' followers are blessed in these ways, the Church community is made visible in the world through their faithfulness. The Church is light to the world and salt to the earth.

This exposition of Matthew, raises important questions, not least for Lutherans, concerning the relation of Christ's teaching and that of the law and the prophets. Jesus was explicit about this, saying, 'Do not think I have come to abolish the law or the prophets; I have come not to abolish but to fulfil' (Matthew 5:17). But, in the wake of the Beatitudes, which despise what the world values and value what the world despises, it can hardly be surprising that the disciples were left wondering if Jesus' teaching separated them not only from the world, but from the law. For Bonhoeffer, it is mistaken both to idolize the law and to legalize God. God is not to be contained by the law any more than God is by doctrine, or the Church, or Scripture. Yet Jesus reaffirms that God gives the law, which is fulfilled in personal fellowship with God. Jesus is not a revolutionary, come to destroy everything that has gone before;' his 'you have heard it said ... but I say to you' is, Bonhoeffer believes, an expression of Jesus' unity with the law and the prophets. Take, for example, the command against adultery. Jesus repeats the command but adds, 'I say to you that everyone who looks at a woman with lust has already committed adultery with her in his heart' (Matthew 5:28). 'At this point', Bonhoeffer asks, must

> we not decisively face the question of whether Jesus intended his command to be taken literally or merely figuratively? Must not our whole life depend on a clear answer to this question? ... If we were to say that, of course, the command is not meant to be taken literally, then we would already have dodged the seriousness of the command. But if we were to say, of course, it should be taken literally, this would only show that Christian existence is absurd on principle, and the command would lose its authority. (*DBW 4* 126)

This is a crucial question for Christian ethics, but particularly for those like Bonhoeffer, who want to connect the New Testament with contemporary moral problems. Yet Bonhoeffer refuses to answer the question, believing that it must be left open because the Bible leaves it open. The crucial thing is simple obedience. He takes a similarly paradoxical approach in interpreting Jesus' injunction against taking oaths ('Jesus rejects lying by prohibiting oaths' *DBW 4* 129); against taking retribution for injustice ('the evil comes to an end when we permit it to pass over us, without defense' *DBW 4* 133); and loving one's enemy (who 'is more worthy of my love than my foe?' *DBW 4* 139).

Where these attitudes are lived fully, believers are distinguished from unbelievers in being 'extraordinary': perfectly pure, truthful, and non-violent. These qualities are visible, but Jesus also warns against practising righteousness before others so that our piety might be admired, and he tells the disciples to pray and fast in secret. Believers in this pattern will discover a renewed zest for life, free from the worry of material acquisition, not because material goods are to be despised – quite the reverse – but because worry betokens a lack of trust in God. This way of life inevitably raises the question of the relation of believers and unbelievers, and Bonhoeffer concludes that the 'call separates a small group, those who follow, from the great mass of the people. The disciples are few and will always be only a few' (*DBW 4* 175). This is the theological foundation for Bonhoeffer's controversial claim that in (Protestant) Germany, there was 'no salvation outside the Confessing Church'. It is encouragement for the Church to be a minority. It is to counter-balance this apparently 'sectarian' turn in his *Discipleship* that Bonhoeffer concluded part one with a brief exposition of Jesus' teaching to the disciples concerning their mission in Matthew chapter 10.

Discipleship and the Church

Part two of *Discipleship*, like part one, begins with the call of Matthew, but now the question raised by it is closer to home:

> Jesus no longer walks past me in bodily form and calls, 'Follow me,' as he did to Levi, the tax collector ... What gives me the right, for example, to hear Jesus' call of the tax collector as being addressed to me? (*DBW 4* 201)

It is the question that has been behind the curtain waiting to make its entrance throughout the whole of part one. But for Bonhoeffer, if Jesus is not dead, but alive and still speaking through the testimony of scripture, he is present for us in body and word just as he was for the first disciples. Today, Christians hear Jesus' call in preaching and sacrament. Baptism is, like Matthew's first step in following Jesus, a visible act of obedience to God's call (and like which, it is something Jesus gives us rather than something we give him). This means it should only be administered where the reality of salvation of which the sacrament speaks can have some hope of being remembered, that is, within the community of faith. For Bonhoeffer, baptizing children of families outside the Church 'betrays reprehensible thoughtlessness' (*DBW 4* 212).

Bonhoeffer is certain that Paul's conviction that the Church is the body of Christ is not merely a colourful or romantic metaphor, for the bodily presence and community of Jesus with the first disciples 'does not mean anything different or anything more than what we have today' (*DBW 4* 213). Feeding off his doctoral dissertation Bonhoeffer's exposition of Pauline ecclesiology reasserts that as the body of Christ the Church is one, but at the same time it is the plurality and community of its members. The Church takes bodily form by being visible in preaching and sacrament. This common life has social implications for Christians, who are not only one at the communion table, but in all their relations with each other. When Philemon was baptized, Paul encouraged him to receive his runaway slave back 'no longer as a slave but ... [as] a beloved brother' (Philemon 16). In the Church social distinctions between slave and free, Jew and Greek are abolished (a daring interpretation, though certainly true, when the Aryan paragraph was willingly being implemented by the 'established' Protestant churches in Germany). Yet, in keeping with Paul's socially conservative attitude in 1 Corinthians 7:20–4, Bonhoeffer repeats that Christians should be content with the social position they held when they were called to discipleship, because Christian freedom is God's gift, irrespective of one's social or political status. Paul's statements are not, Bonhoeffer clarifies, 'a justification or a Christian apology for a shadowy social order' (*DBW 4* 238); renouncing political rebellion is an expression of Christian hope, which lies in God, and not in any political solution that the world can offer. Christians are, as Paul teaches in Romans 13, to obey the governing authorities not in order to gain advantage for the Church (e.g. security or respectability or influence) but in obedience to God's order. It is perhaps telling that, when making his defence to the examining magistrate after his arrest, Bonhoeffer referred to this passage in *Discipleship* to help bolster the image he was attempting to paint of himself as a loyal citizen!

The disciples are not subject to the world, but they live within it. By this, Bonhoeffer continues, he means that the Church 'is a territory with an authority of its own, a space set apart' (*DBW 4* 253). It is important to pause on this phrase, which represents a concluding moment in the argument of *Discipleship*. In the mid-1930s, Bonhoeffer committed considerable thought and energy to carving out a space for the Confessing Church within the 'established' Protestant churches in Germany, in relation to the Nazi state, and, internationally, within the nascent worldwide fellowship of churches. As it turned out, this proved to be very largely a losing battle. Partly in consequence of his experiences, but more, I suspect, as his theological ethics matured, Bonhoeffer began to see considerable danger in speaking as if there was either a metaphorical or a physical space that is 'Church' in relation to an entirely separate space that is 'world'. In his *Ethics* he would call this 'thinking in two spheres'. For our purposes, it provides a stark spatial image of what has been a strong theme throughout *Discipleship*: namely the distinctiveness or extraordinariness of Christians vis-à-vis unbelievers. In prison, Bonhoeffer's last word on *Discipleship* would be that 'I thought I could acquire faith by trying to live a holy life, or something like it. I suppose I wrote *Discipleship* as the end of that path. Today I can see the dangers of that book, though I still stand by what I wrote' (*LPP* 369, tr. amended). Too much can be read into this passing comment (and indeed has been) but we are sure that Bonhoeffer came to suspect the theological sense in expressing the distinctiveness of the disciples spatially. For our purposes, an equally intriguing question is whether Bonhoeffer had come to 'see the dangers' of the *ethics* of *Discipleship*. If Bonhoeffer lost confidence in the spatial distinctiveness of the Church community, did his confidence waver in the moral visibility and distinctiveness of the disciple? There is little evidence that it did. However, as we have already observed, Bonhoeffer certainly reappraised elements in *Discipleship* ethics: he reinterpreted the command to love one's enemy in the context of the conspiracy. In *Discipleship* Bonhoeffer condemns perjury, but in his essay on telling the truth (which we will touch upon in the next chapter) he conceives of circumstances in which truthfulness will mean telling lies, even under oath. And in wartime Germany, Bonhoeffer interpreted Paul's teaching that 'there is no authority except from God' (Romans 13:1b) by praying and working for the defeat of his country. Bonhoeffer intentionally left some ethical questions unanswered in his book (e.g. whether Jesus' commands are to be understood literally or figuratively). But does he leave other, crucial questions unanswered or unasked? He argues forcefully that Christian ethics are distinct: but then, how is the believer to incorporate into Christian ethics the values and perspectives she has gained from without the church community, for example in the family? He argues that we must leave open the possibility that the divine command contained in the law and fulfilled in Christ are to be answered literally, but he did not suggest adulterers be executed (Leviticus 20:10), he ate pork in literal disobedience of the law (Leviticus 11:8), and presumably kept his money in an interest bearing bank account (Deuteronomy 23:19). Bonhoeffer acknowledges that it is because of the 'absurdity' involved in literal obedience to the law that a 'paradoxical' interpretation of the law is necessary; but resort to paradox is rarely if ever satisfactory, and it is no more so here. Bonhoeffer says I must obey simply, and that if I ask 'yes, but *which* commandments do I keep and which do I abandon?' I follow in the disobedient slither marks of the serpent and the sad footsteps of the rich young ruler. His statement has very considerable rhetorical and homiletic force; but how does it help me if, in spite of his insistence that obedience is always simple, I still cannot see what God wants me to do?

Life Together

If *Discipleship* is a product of Bonhoeffer's attempt to train clergy for the Confessing Church, then *Life Together* is a product of his 'experiments' in community life in the seminary, but more particularly in the Brothers' House that tried to offer a model of community life for the other students, and for the Church. It is perhaps unfair to call the patterns of community life developed by Bonhoeffer 'experiments' – both the seminary and the Brothers' House achieved what Bonhoeffer wanted for them, and their closure was not due to intrinsic flaws in either community. But while some churches had practised forms of communal living for generations, living communally was a new and daring departure for Lutherans, who after all were named after a man who had left a Christian community to reform the Church.

Life Together, according to its author, is 'a look at several directions and principles that the Holy Scriptures give us for life together under the Word (*DBW 5* 27). Living the Christian life together with others is a privilege that is not afforded to every believer. So when a believer can share his faith daily with others it is a source of incomparable joy and strength. A Christian needs other Christians for Jesus' sake and indeed is only able to be joined with them in community through Christ. Christian community depends on God: it is chosen and accepted by God in time, and its eternal unity is to be found in Christ. Bonhoeffer believes that if these insights are taken seriously it becomes possible to grasp that Christian community is not an ideal of some kind, but is a 'divine reality', by which, he explains, it is important to understand that Christian community is a spiritual rather than a psychic reality. Sooner or later, anyone living within a Christian community becomes disillusioned with others in it, with herself or even with God. If Christian community were an idealized form of human community, such disillusionment would be able to kill community off. But because Christian community is a God-given reality, the faults of others in my congregation or community (or indeed my own faults) serve to remind me of our mutual dependence on forgiveness of sin in Jesus Christ. Likewise, Christian community could not hope to flourish if it were merely tasked with satisfying the psychic, natural emotional urges, strengths and weaknesses of the human soul. A surprising number of Christians think that Christian community serves just these purposes – to satisfy one's emotional needs in worship and fellowship, or to give one a sense of belonging. But within a spiritual Christian community members do not set out with the presumption that community is there to meet their own needs, but as a place that affords them the privilege of meeting the needs of others. The contrast is marked strongly in terms of the love a member of a Christian community shows:

> Self-centered love constructs its own image of other persons, about what they are and what they should become. It takes the life of the other person into its own hands. Spiritual love recognizes the true image of the other person seen from the perspective of Jesus Christ. It is the image Jesus Christ has formed and wants to form in all people. (*DBW 5* 44)

For a Christian community the day begins at dawn in common worship. Whatever an individual or the whole community may be worried about in the coming day the first moment of the day ought to be free from worry because it belongs to God, to whom life belongs. Worship will include Bible reading, song and prayer. A psalm will be said. A substantial reading of Scripture should follow – a chapter from the Old Testament and half a chapter from the New Testament – from a lectionary that reads the Bible in a consecutive cycle, so that over time the whole of the Bible is heard by the community. Reading the Church's Scripture together, the community is caught up in the biblical stories, and above all into the life of Jesus, and so participates in these healing events of baptism, teaching, death and resurrection. Singing is the community's response to these gifts. Worship concludes in prayer for the community and the world, and, Bonhoeffer asserts, should be spoken extempore (rather than from a written prayer) by the 'head' of the community. Set prayers can certainly help, but they can be an evasion from real prayer where they are beautiful and profound, but not genuinely spoken. Only then may the community eat breakfast together. Eating together is an important symbol of Christian community: Jesus ate daily meals with his disciples and also shared with them in his last supper. Today, the Christian community continues to share in both forms of fellowship and, in the breaking of bread, its eyes are opened to see Jesus (Luke 24:30–31a). From this point of the day, until the community meets again in worship at dusk, the day belongs to work. It is important to distinguish prayer and work, so that prayer does not get in the way of work, or work in the way of prayer.

Community life has its temptations, among the strongest of which is that people who are incapable of being alone turn to community as an artificial protection against loneliness. For Bonhoeffer, a correlation exists between one's capacity to be in community and to be alone, such that 'Whoever cannot be alone should beware of community ... [and] Whoever cannot stand being in community should beware of being alone' (*DBW* 5 82). At significant moments and in key Christian and human events, every individual stands alone; we are alone in the decision to follow Jesus; we are alone in confronting death. Being alone is not, therefore, something to avoid, but to welcome. But our calling is also always a calling to community life, and in another sense, even in death and facing God's judgement, we stand with others in an eternal community of faith. The mark of life alone is silence, which can be experienced as terror and isolation, as the perfect setting for self-deception, but also as the place of simple encounter with the Word of God. To structure time alone properly, a Christian should make room for a daily time of meditation in which to read Scripture, pray and intercede in prayer for others. While the Bible reading together should be relatively long, there is sense in making the Bible passages one reads alone short. By 'intercession' Bonhoeffer means 'Christians bringing one another into the presence of God, seeing each other under the cross of Jesus as poor human beings and sinners in need of grace' (*DBW* 5 90). It is through intercessory prayer that Christians seek for others that which they themselves are graced with: the right to stand before Christ and to share in his mercy.

Arguments can destroy community. Yet it is almost inevitable that any gathering of human beings will hold within it scope for disagreement. People are extraordinarily varied, in talent, ability, temperament, need and strength. In the Christian community, the tongue must be disciplined, and one believer must not speak badly of another. When an attempt is made to follow this principle, it can be very liberating, as it means one is not always on the look out for fault. Positively, the proper attitude of the Christian community is one of service. This means listening genuinely and unreservedly to other members of the community. It means offering help in practical ways, however 'humble' the act of service may be. And it means being patient with others in a Christian community, bearing with them however much someone may grate on us. This will normally take the form of forgiving the other wordlessly in prayer. These acts alone create the circumstances in which it may be possible to serve another by offering God's word. Jesus, Bonhoeffer believes, tied authority in the community to service, so that only where an authorized person listens, helps, forbears and proclaims God's Word is his authority properly established. His abilities and talents are of no significance in community, and may even poison it by setting himself rather than Christ at the centre of the community. The authority of the community's leader therefore rests on the same basis as the obedience of those with whom he exercises it, in the authority of the Word.

The last chapter of *Life Together* culminates in 'confession and the Lord's Supper', in which Bonhoeffer details the controversial practice in the seminary and in the Brothers' House of mutual confession. 'When I go to another believer to confess', Bonhoeffer states calmly, 'I am going to God. Thus the call within the Christian community to mutual confession and forgiveness goes out as a call to the great grace of God in the congregation' (*DBW* 5 109). Any Christian believer – not the ordained alone – may hear confession, Bonhoeffer believes. There is every difference between revealing oneself in confession to a fellow Christian, and revealing oneself to a psychologist or analyst. Because sin is different to sickness, another believer 'views me as I am before the judging and merciful God in the cross of Jesus Christ' (*DBW* 5 115). Such confession is, in the Christian community, an essential preparation for the Lord's Supper, which is the joy and destination of the Christian community.

Life Together makes a distinctive contribution to our under-standing of Bonhoeffer's theological ethics: it shows how they are rooted for the Christian in an individual and communal life of prayer and worship. The shaping and patterning of a Christian orientation towards others arises from participation in the common Christian life, with all its frustrations and hard knocks. The attitudes and perspectives that give direction to Christian ethics do not, therefore, come from skilled study or intellectual brilliance: they are gifts of God made to believers when they pray, read scripture 'spiritually', confess, and celebrate the Lord's Supper. Nowhere is this significant note sounded with such clarity as it is here, but it is an unspoken presupposition of all Bonhoeffer's ethics.

Notes

1   See *Caravaggio: A life*, Helen Langdon, Chatto & Windus, London, 1998, for both a biography of the artist and commentary on *The call of St Matthew*.

2   '... [I]t is impossible to write about Caravaggio without using theatrical metaphors'. *Painting the Word*, John Drury, Yale University Press, 1999, p. 124.

3   Published in New York by Harper and Brothers, 1935.

4   It is quite possible that Karl Barth's use of this New Testament incident in the *Church Dogmatics II/2*, pp. 613–30, owes a debt to Bonhoeffer's exegesis. The story of the rich young ruler forms the basis too for Pope John Paul II's 1993 Encyclical *Veritatis Splendor*, which, though it does not mention Barth, can hardly have been ignorant of his use of the story since they are so similar.

5   Bonhoeffer's repeated insistence that Jesus is not a revolutionary, and his earlier dismissal of 'programmes of social action' should give pause to anyone seeking to find in Bonhoeffer's theology a prototype for Liberation Theology.

7

The ethics of responsible action

Ethics in crisis: a stock-take of Bonhoeffer's theology

It seems unnecessary to say that Europe under Nazi rule was in moral crisis. When Bonhoeffer began work on his *Ethics* the German army had invaded Czechoslovakia and Poland and its plans to invade other countries were ready to be put into action. As he wrote, the German state initiated a programme of 'euthanasia' aimed at 'removing the burden' of those with mental illness or mental disability from the German people. He was still writing as the Final Solution of the 'Jewish problem' got under way. To say Europe needed more or better ethics was surely to do no more than state the obvious. Yet for Bonhoeffer the moral crisis that met the eye so appallingly in Nazi Germany was an outcrop of a more disturbing crisis in human ethics. Bonhoeffer's *Ethics* addresses a crisis that predates Nazi rule, and even predates the Enlightenment, with which more recent moral diagnosticians have been concerned.[1] The Nazis had brought Europe's moral calamity to a head; but because it went deeper than Nazi misrule and criminality it would not dissipate when the Nazis were consigned to the dustbin of history.

Bonhoeffer's sense of moral crisis had been growing for years. In *Sanctorum Communio* he had challenged the prevailing liberal consensus by emphasizing the ecclesial and community dimension of life. Liberal theology had forgotten the truth that the Church can only be fully understood by those within it. Liberal culture had gone too far in individualizing ethics and the life of faith. All theological concepts, Bonhoeffer asserted, are social. In particular sin is social, since it disrupts social relations between people as well as the relation of human beings with God. Ethics is not simply a matter for private reflection and decision; it is central to the life of a community. In *Act and Being* Bonhoeffer transposed his conviction that the Church can only be properly understood by its members into a study of the theory of knowledge. How can we know God? Is God revealed in discrete acts of revelation alone, or does God somehow *exist*, 'haveable' and graspable in the world? An answer to these questions, he wrote, can only be found amongst those to whom God has already given Godself. As in his earlier dissertation, though he did not spell it out ethically, his argument had ethical implications. For Christians to know what to do depends on them being able truly to know what God wills; and that depends on the possibility of revelation. Revelation only makes sense, he proposed, if it is both act and being; both a matter of what God does directly, here and now and of God's longer term being with us, Emmanuel! Deeds and character cohere in God, and through faith cohere also in the believer.

In *Creation and Fall* Bonhoeffer developed in full his understanding of the Fall and of the sinfulness of humanity. The Apostle Paul had written that though he wanted to do good, something in his human nature prevented him from actually doing the good he willed to do. In *Creation and Fall,* Bonhoeffer 'named' the reason for a human incapacity to act according to good intentions in the rich biblical imagery of the Fall of Adam. Ethics, Bonhoeffer explained, derive from the Fall; the knowledge of good and evil at the heart of ethical debate is a consequence of eating the fruit of the tree of knowledge of good and evil. Ethics is, therefore, a symptom of loss at the Fall of humankind's original unity with God. The ethical question 'what is the right thing to do?' did not exist until the Fall because Adam and Eve simply knew and obeyed God's will for them. In his christology lectures Bonhoeffer described the point at which a recovery of that unity begins: not in speculative theological debates, or by somehow repristinating impure doctrine; but by asking 'who is Jesus Christ for me?' *Discipleship* pressed ·the distinctive character of the Christian life to its fullest extent in the language of costly grace and discipleship, and in both *Discipleship* and *Life Together,* Bonhoeffer gave concrete shape to individual and communal Christian life. *Life Together* spelled out for a popular readership the commitment to the Church community with which Bonhoeffer's career began.

In his writings prior to 1939 Bonhoeffer had wrestled with ecclesiology, epistemology, soteriology and christology. He had developed an unusual biblical hermeneutic. But though he had raised ethical issues in each of his earlier writings, prior to 1939 he had not worked his theology through explicitly in terms of ethics. In this chapter I want to see what these themes look like when seen from the perspective of ethics. How is the question of the distinctiveness of Christian life and knowledge worked through in ethics? How should we express ethically the 'haveable', graspable presence of God in both act and being? What concrete practical forms might the good life take? But before turning to these questions it is necessary to pause on the textual and hermeneutical problems of Bonhoeffer's *Ethics*.

Excursion: difficulties with reading Bonhoeffer's *Ethics*

Bonhoeffer's *Ethics* is a difficult text. In his preface to the first edition of the *Ethics* in 1949,[2] Eberhard Bethge observed that 'This is not the *Ethics* which Dietrich Bonhoeffer intended to publish ... The material has come to us in such a form that there has been no possibility of working out a clear arrangement of the extant chapters ...' The manuscripts from which Bethge compiled the *Ethics* have all the signs of being in draft form: crossings out, new paragraphs interleaved with older material and rewrites of earlier sections. In addition there are hundreds of scraps of paper on which Bonhoeffer wrote notes for his book, including a draft outline, from which he later departed. Only a letter tentatively suggests a possible title for the book, 'Preparing the way and entering upon it'.[3] In the second edition (1963), in part using ink and paper types as evidence, Bethge rearranged the fragments according to a theory that there were four clear starting points in the essays. He included an appendix of ethical material written contemporaneously with the ethics, but not intended as part of it. In the most recent edition (*DBWG 7*) the editors have pursued this approach to dating the manuscripts of the *Ethics* with even greater rigour and submit, more or less unanimously, a new and 'definitive' chronological ordering of the *Ethics*. They propose that there were five periods of time during which Bonhoeffer worked on his *Ethics*, for some of which there is surer evidence than others. Essays written in a particular period often form a clearly recognizable and self-consistent block. In addition to this chronological ordering of the manuscripts, the editors also suggest a hypothetical reconstruction of the *Ethics* fragments as Bonhoeffer *might* have ordered them.

It makes sense to suppose that the sequence in which one reads the essays in Bonhoeffer's *Ethics* makes a difference to how one understands them. If we try to read them in the sequence Bonhoeffer may have intended them to be read, we might, for example, have a stronger sense of a progression in his argument. Or, if we pay heed to the context of each essay, the *sitz im leben* of a text, we may be more aware of the circumstances on Bonhoeffer's mind and the way they shape what he writes. For example, knowing that the section of the *Ethics* on euthanasia was a response to information passed to Bonhoeffer on the Nazi euthanasia programme helps to account for its clarity and passion. The hypothetical reconstruction is based on good evidence and is persuasive though necessarily speculative. Certainly the textual evidence should be attended to as far as possible. But the *Ethics* are still best read as a fragmentary collection of essays and taken as such at face value. I have sometimes tracked themes drawn from material found in several essays, but in a later section of this chapter, headed 'Character and command', I contrast the approach to ethics of two particularly well-defined periods of writing.

The distinctive nature of Christian ethics

What are Christian ethics? Bonhoeffer begins two separate sections of the *Ethics* – 'Christ, reality and the good' and 'The love of God and the decay of the world' – by considering this question. In 'Christ, reality and the good', probably written between the summer and the autumn of 1940, Bonhoeffer distinguishes the starting point of Christian ethics from those of all other secular and religious ethics.

> Whoever wishes to take up the problem of a Christian ethic ... must from the outset discard as irrelevant the two questions which alone impel him to concern himself with the problem of ethics, 'How can I be good?' and 'How can I do good?', and instead of these he must ask the utterly and totally different question, 'What is the will of God?' (*E* 161)

If ethics truly were a matter of my goodness and of making the world good through my actions, then I would be the ultimate reality, the centre of the universe! In the sharpest contrast, Christian ethics sets out from the claim that both 'I' and 'my' world are embedded in the ultimate reality of God, who alone is creator, reconciler and redeemer. The aim of Christian ethics then becomes 'the realization of the revelational reality of God in Christ'. The only good that matters – the only goal to which ethics should aim – is therefore human participation in the reality of God. Bonhoeffer understood that this definition of ethics sets Christian ethics in a polemical relationship to all other ethics. In the opening paragraphs of 'The love of God and the decay of the world', probably written in the second half of 1942, he candidly states that:

> The knowledge of good and evil seems to be the aim of all ethical reflection. The first task of Christian ethics is to invalidate this knowledge ... Christian ethics claims to discuss the origin of the whole problem of ethics, and thus professes to be a critique of all ethics simply as ethics. (*E* 3)

Already in the opening paragraphs of these two essays, Bonhoeffer introduces concepts key to his book. Picking up the insights of *Creation and Fall*, he first characterizes ethics as a recovery of the unity of God and humanity, and the unity between human beings, disrupted by the Fall. If knowledge of good and evil comes at the expense of unity with God, then even conscience, typically regarded by ethicists as an instrument of good, is a sign of disunity with God. For this reason Bonhoeffer calls for Christian ethics, in Nietzsche's phrase, to go 'beyond good and evil'. For Nietzsche, good and evil were part of what he called a 'slave morality'. His philosophy – he called it 'a prelude to the future' – envisaged a liberated élite who would live beyond good and evil by creating their own morality that would be generous and benevolent towards those who were weaker. Bonhoeffer shared Nietzsche's wariness of the pettiness of many moral conventions and admired him for his boldness. But while Nietzsche held that freedom could be seized by strong individuals, Bonhoeffer believed true freedom lay in accepting one's creatureliness before God. Only in the New Testament is the world of recovered unity possible. In contrast with the Pharisee, who is a man of conscience, and therefore one who lives life in disunion with his origin, Jesus 'lives and acts not by the knowledge of good and evil but by the will of God. There is only one will of God. In it the origin is recovered; in it there is established the freedom and the simplicity of all action' (*E* 15). This is the meaning of Jesus' saying 'judge not, that ye be not judged'.

When the original unity of God's creation was sundered by the Fall, reality itself, Bonhoeffer continues, was torn apart. Ethics became a matter of 'thinking in two spheres'. On the one hand was the holy, the supernatural and Christian; on the other was the worldly, the profane and the natural. People faced a choice about which sphere they belonged to: the spiritual or the secular. The result was that though a small number in monastic communities could claim to live spiritually, most people were consigned to life in the secular sphere. Bonhoeffer was sure that this way of conceiving matters was profoundly unbiblical; that is, in the Bible, thinking of reality in two spheres was unknown. 'Sharing in Christ', he explained, 'we stand at once in both the reality of God and the reality of the world' (*E* 170). To be sure, the Christian is not identical with the world, nor the natural with the supernatural; 'but between the two there is in each case a unity which derives solely from the reality of Christ' *(E* 171).

To find a way of speaking faithfully of the unity of reality, and yet of maintaining a proper sense of the tension between the Christian and the world, the natural and the supernatural, Bonhoeffer developed a vocabulary of 'the ultimate and the penultimate'. At several points in this book we have asked whether Bonhoeffer's strong convictions about the distinctiveness of Christian theology, knowledge and ethics, does not make it difficult for Christians to engage with reality. In his categories of the penultimate and the ultimate, he offers his strongest explanation yet of how Christians are in but not of the world. Ultimately, Christians are justified by grace and faith alone. But how are these ultimate truths realizable in the messiness of penultimate, everyday life? The best way to show what is at stake is to take a concrete example. When a Christian stands by someone in despair, for example someone recently bereaved, she has available to her ultimate words of comfort – the promise of salvation, the promise of resurrection. But Bonhoeffer's experience as a Pastor led him to think that it is often better for a time simply to keep silence with the grieving person. 'Does one not in some cases, by remaining deliberately in the penultimate, perhaps point all the more genuinely to the ultimate, which God will speak in his own time?' (*E* 104). Certainly, ultimate gospel truths of hope and resurrection, faith and love, constitute a judgement on everything in the world that is not at all or not fully in keeping with them. Yet the judgement of these ultimate truths on the penultimate is tempered with mercy, for the penultimate reality of the world belongs to God too. The penultimate world is not annulled by the ultimate, indeed 'for the sake of the ultimate the penultimate must be preserved' (*E* 111).

In his prison letters Bonhoeffer would write that 'we live in the last but one and believe the last, don't we? ... But the logical conclusions are far reaching, e.g. for the problem of Catholicism, for the concept of the ministry, for the use of the Bible, etc., and above all for ethics' (*LPP* 157). So what are the consequences for ethics? Bonhoeffer again uses a simple illustration to make his point. 'If the hungry man does not attain to faith, then the guilt falls on those who refused him bread' (*E* 114). Providing bread to the hungry, justice for the dispossessed, a roof for the homeless, or fellowship for the lonely, does not amount to giving the ultimate gifts of justification and faith: they are penultimate gifts. But these penultimate gifts prepare the way – an echo of Bonhoeffer's proposed title for his book – for Christ. It is in this sense of 'preparing the way' that the penultimate is related to the ultimate. This positive way of speaking of the penultimate shows that it is a mistake to be satisfied with penultimate things, as if by contenting ourselves with giving penultimate things we have done enough. After all, the way of grace is not conditional upon the fulfilment of material liberties or rights. Moreover, a man may spend himself caring for the needy and remain a sinner. Nevertheless 'it still makes a difference whether the penultimate is attended to and taken seriously or not' (*E* 116). Ultimately, doing good won't save you – or those to whom good is done – but God still wills us to do good things because it prepares the way for grace.

Nature and ethics

The recovery of the penultimate for ethics led Bonhoeffer towards a reappraisal of the natural. Catholic theology and ethics, Bonhoeffer believed, had retained a capacity for reflection upon natural life, nature, and natural theology that Protestant ethics had lost. The Protestant emphasis on the sinfulness of humanity and creation virtually reduced Protestant ethics to the condemnation of sin. Bonhoeffer had never shared the knee-jerk antipathy to Catholicism of many Lutherans and the section of his *Ethics* dedicated to 'the natural', written during a long winter stay at a Catholic monastery in Ettal, is sympathetically oriented to Catholic moral theology. 'The concept of the natural must, therefore,' he wrote, 'be recovered on the basis of the gospel ... The natural is that which, after the Fall, is directed towards the coming of Christ. The unnatural is that which, after the Fall, closes its doors against the coming of Christ' (*E* 120–1). The natural corresponds to the penultimate; which means that the natural life is a preliminary to life with Christ. The natural life has a certain independence from God, a life of its own that is guaranteed by God in order that those who live naturally may be led towards the ultimate life in Christ. On this basis and to this penultimate extent, human beings may be said to have natural rights. These include the right to bodily life. Harming someone's body, injuring or killing another person, is wrong because it infringes this right. This rule has exceptions – Bonhoeffer includes punishment of criminals – but all arbitrary taking of life is wrong, and '[a]ll deliberate killing of innocent life is arbitrary' (*E* 135). Context is all-important at this point in the *Ethics* as Bonhoeffer, with the Nazis' euthanasia programme in mind, makes it axiomatic that 'the right to life takes precedence over the right to kill' (*E* 137). To be sure, a distinction can be made morally between killing, and allowing a patient to die. But in this case, the patient's interests are all that matters. The interests of society as a whole, for example the cost to society of keeping a patient alive indefinitely, cannot be taken into account, since it is false to assume that the value of life consists only in its usefulness to society. By and large, the natural right to bodily life also makes suicide wrong. 'God has reserved to Himself the right to determine the end of life, because He alone knows the goal to which it is His will to lead it' (*E* 143). Yet Bonhoeffer admits exceptions: if a prisoner takes his life (again it is important to recall the context) for fear that under torture he might betray his country, his family, or his friend, condemnation of the deed becomes impossible. Similarly, Bonhoeffer sets out in relation to the ethics of reproduction, contraception and abortion with a premiss in favour of the right to bodily life, but grants that 'scope must . . . be allowed for the free action of a conscience which renders account to God' (*E* 153).[4] With a certain unintended symbolism, Bonhoeffer did not complete his essay on the natural: the task of rendering a satisfactory account of the natural in the context of Protestant ethics is likewise incomplete.

Character and command: two 'moods' in which to do ethics

How should we express ethically the 'haveable', graspable presence of God in both act and being? In Chapter 4 we read Bonhoeffer's early theology in the light of contemporary discussion of the relative moral priority of the individual and of society. *Sanctorum*

Communio answered that question in terms of 'both/and' rather than 'either/or'. In *Act and Being*, Bonhoeffer again resisted an artificially sharp choice, as he saw it, between viewing revelation either in terms of act or in terms of being. A second contemporary debate, concerning the relation of doing good and being good, of moral action versus moral character, provided a context in which to understand what was at stake. In two sections of Bonhoeffer's *Ethics,* both debates resurface with renewed vigour and clarity. In 'Ethics as formation', written in the second half of 1940, and 'The ethical and the Christian as a theme', written in early 1943, Bonhoeffer presents us with the ethical equivalents of being-based theology and act-based theology. The themes explored in these sections can be expressed as sharp alternatives, just as act and being can be expressed as sharp alternatives. 'Is ethics all about the conditions necessary for shaping good character (being); or is it rather simply a matter of obeying God's commands (acts)?' But the temptation – for that is what it is – to interpret ethics as formation and ethics as command as two alternative approaches to ethics is resisted by Bonhoeffer. Just as Bonhoeffer attempted to reconcile act and being, so in his *Ethics* he sets out to reconcile formation and command. It is a task of considerable contemporary relevance.

To help make this case I want to suggest a metaphor that uses the word 'mood' in its grammatical sense. In grammar, 'mood' denotes the form or set of forms of a verb that serves to indicate if it expresses a fact (the indicative mood); a command (the imperative mood); a question (the interrogative mood); the conditions for what is imagined, wished, or possible (the subjunctive mood); a call (the vocative mood); or a wish (the optative mood). David Ford finds all these moods in Bonhoeffer's theology, and employs a metaphor from Bonhoeffer's prison letters to speak of 'the polyphony of Christian life.[5] Two of these 'moods' are extremely helpful as a means of describing Bonhoeffer's two leading approaches to ethics as formation and command. Though there are significant themes in many sections of Bonhoeffer's *Ethics*, only in these two sections is there what can be called an explicit method.[6]

Ethics as formation is ethics conducted in the subjunctive mood. The subjunctive mood describes the mood of a verb in which the speaker states a relation she wishes for between the subject and the predicate (grammatical examples are 'if I were you' and 'God help you'). In my use of this 'mood metaphor', ethics in the subjunctive mood is one in which the ethicist wishes for a particular relation between the ethical subject and the person of Christ. If Bonhoeffer was interested in the character of ethics, he was also interested in the ethics of character. '*Gestaltung*', the German word translated as 'formation', normally refers to a spatial form; but it can also mean a character in a play, and thereby 'character' in the context of morality. 'Today', Bonhoeffer writes, 'there are once more villains and saints, and they are not hidden from the public view … Shakespeare's characters (*Gestalten*) walk in our midst' (*E* 46). Such characters, Bonhoeffer continues, teach us that ethics is not simply concerned with individual sins or good deeds, but with underlying moral character. 'What is worse than doing evil is being evil. It is worse for a liar to tell the truth than for a lover of truth to lie. It is worse when a misanthropist practices brotherly love than when a philanthropist gives way to hatred' (*E* 46–7). In short, falling away from being good is far more serious than making a one-off mistake. Deeds are ethically insignificant besides questions of moral identity. The character of the Christian must therefore take on the form, that is the *Gestalt*, of Jesus Christ who John the Baptist welcomed with the words '*Ecce homo*', behold the man. In a beautiful passage, Bonhoeffer offers a character description of the Christ to whom the Christian is conformed. He is the reconciler; he is the one who truly loves men and women; he is the true man who takes on himself the guilt of the world who is sentenced and executed; he is the Risen man. All this is in contrast with the values prominent in the German society that Bonhoeffer challenges in which enemies are despised, success lionized and death idolized. Bonhoeffer concludes that 'formation comes only by being drawn into the form of Jesus Christ. It comes only as formation in His likeness, as *conformation* with the unique form of him who was made man, was crucified, and rose again' (*E* 61). Because Jesus was incarnate, the purpose of this conformation is not to become divine, but to learn what it means to be properly human. Because he is the Crucified, the conformation means bearing with Jesus the suffering of the world and the judgement of God. Because conformation is to the Risen One, it means becoming a new creature, life in the midst of death. Bonhoeffer's 'ethics as formation' predates what theologians have learned to speak of as 'narrative theology', but his *Ethics* at this point is strikingly suggestive of the insight of narrative theologians that human life is story-formed. Bonhoeffer insists that for the Christian, ethical life means forming oneself on the 'story-form' character of Jesus. 'Ethics as formation' is ethics in the subjunctive mood, ethics conditional upon a formation to Christ's character. It is an ethical version of 'If I were You …'.

In contrast, 'ethics as command' suggests the imperative mood. 'The "ethical" and the Christian as a theme' was the last section of the *Ethics* written before Bonhoeffer's arrest. Bonhoeffer rules out any approach to ethics based on timeless eternally valid moral principles or rules. Why is it, he asks, that ethics usually crosses our minds when we face difficult decisions? It is because only where community is disrupted is the 'you shall' of ethics perceived in its most acute form. Earlier, he has suggested that moral decisions are most difficult when they reach us not as simple choices between a right and a wrong, but in the complex form of a choice between two rights, or two wrongs. In such instances, where the right course of action is not self-evident, ethical reflection still serves a useful purpose. Even so, it is easier to say what an ethic is not than what it is: 'An ethic cannot be a book', Bonhoeffer writes, 'in which there is set out how everything in the world actually ought to be but unfortunately is not; and an ethicist cannot be a person who always knows better than others what is to be done'. (*E* 236) [translation amended]

In response, Bonhoeffer introduces the concept of a warrant for ethical statements. This warrant is an authority to speak ethically. It is not based on merit, but on the position a warrant holder has in relation to another. The pastor has a warrant in relation to his congregation, a parent to his child, a magistrate to his citizens. The order in their relationship is not arbitrary, but rests for Bonhoeffer, on the command of God:

> The commandment of God is something different from what we have so far referred to as the ethical. It embraces the whole of life. It is not only unconditional; it is also total. It does not only forbid and command; it also permits. It does not only bind; it also sets free; and it does this by binding. Yet the 'ethical', in a sense which still has to be explained, is part of it. God's commandment is the only warrant for ethical discourse. (*E* 244)

For Bonhoeffer, the divine command is therefore not a concrete set of timeless moral principles. God's commandment is the speech of God that, in both its content and in its form, is God's concrete word to a particular person at a particular moment. Its central feature is that 'God's commandment leaves man no room for application or interpretation' (*E* 245). Bonhoeffer does not mean that the hearer plays no role in acting on the command, as though she were a puppet on a string, but that when God commands God leaves room only for obedience or disobedience. The question 'what does God command?' is the ethical echo of the serpent's question in Eden 'did God really say?' If one has to ask the question, one has not heard God's command. In 1939 Bonhoeffer did not have to ask 'what is the right thing to do, stay in America or return to Germany?' He knew God was commanding him to be in Germany. His choice was simply to obey or disobey.

It is significant that the section of the *Ethics* concerned with command was among the last to be written. The text breaks off suddenly and the manuscript lay on Bonhoeffer's desk the day he was arrested. Clifford Green observes that it sounds like a fresh start inspired by Karl Barth. It is not so much a radical departure from the ideas of the second block as an experiment in the foundations of Christian ethics based on the distinction and relation of the "ethical" and the "commandment of God".[7] If it had been written first, because of its similarity of content and tone to *Discipleship* (in particular in the prominence given to the idea of simple obedience) it might have been dismissed as a last remnant of an earlier approach to ethics, abandoned as Bonhoeffer's thinking matured. Setting Bonhoeffer's command based ethics alongside his ethics as formation, enables us to see these ethical 'methods' as two sides of a dialectic: the one concerned with being in Christ (conformation to the *Gestalt* of Jesus), the other concerned to emphasize God's freedom to command particular things to particular people (God's freedom to act).

In spite of the balance created by Bonhoeffer's dialectical method, his theology of command poses problems. Christian history is littered with people who have claimed direct revelation from God. The Zwickau prophets challenged Luther's authority by their claim to have received a revelation from God; Kierkegaard found himself baffled with Adolph Adler's claim to have heard God speaking directly to him; Bishop Butler turned up his nose at the early Methodists whose claim of special revelations he found 'a very horrid thing'. Are we really to accept that everyone who claims a divine revelation has actually received one? What are we to make of Bonhoeffer's view that God commands and that all we must do is obey or disobey? Bonhoeffer, like Kierkegaard and Luther before him, understood perfectly that this way of putting things creates a problem: ethics based on God's commandments raise the very difficult question of how one distinguishes between the mad and the holy, between the fanatic and the disciple. The Nazis claimed that Hitler was a messenger of God for the German *Volk*; the conspirators heard God's command to kill him. Who is to umpire such conflict? In his theology of the divine mandates, Bonhoeffer attempts a partial, penultimate answer to questions concerning the concrete form taken by divine command in the day-to-day world.

A divine mandate is a staking out of a 'space' where it is possible to hear the divine command clearly. In the *Ethics* Bonhoeffer has two slightly different attempts at 'naming' divine mandates. In unpacking his theology of command he names four mandates: Church, marriage and the family, culture and government. Earlier in his manuscripts he wrote that four mandates could be gleaned from the Bible, listing these as 'labour, marriage, government and the Church'. In prison he wondered if friendship might be a subdivision of the mandate of culture, or if the brotherhood of the Church, or the comradeship of labour might be mandates. Bonhoeffer's mandates theology was a work in progress and the four mandates he names should be thought of as examples of what he had in mind rather than an exhaustive list. Even so, Bonhoeffer's essential idea is clear enough: the mandates exist for both Christian and non-Christian in society. They provide a system of checks and balances that serves to afford each individual mandate its proper sphere of influence and helps to prevent any single mandate (e.g. government) becoming too dominant over the others (e.g. family). The relationship between the mandates is thus essential to their health. If the mandates limit each other's authority, ultimately, God sets further limits. The inner life of a mandate is bounded by authority, as within each mandate some are given responsibility to lead and others an obligation to be led.

Bonhoeffer's theology of the divine mandates is one of the twentieth-century's most striking theological legitimations of political authority. When Barth reflected on Bonhoeffer's mandates theology, he wondered if there was not 'just a suggestion of North German Patriarchalism' in them and asked, 'is the notion of authority as some over others really more characteristic of the ethical event than that of the freedom of even the very lowest before the very highest?'[8] Yet in spite of his reservations, Barth still saw greater merit in Bonhoeffer's reworking of the 'orders of creation' than in other contemporaneous attempts by Lutheran theologians to rework Luther's teaching on the 'orders of creation'. In the best known of these, Emil Brunner proposed 'orders' that were independent of divine authority. This 'independence' was theologically intolerable for Bonhoeffer, who wanted to base the mandates in God's authoritative command (a link made plain in English by the etymological relationship of 'command' and 'mandate').

In an essay probably written by Bonhoeffer in prison, and certainly with an eye to his interrogation, we gain an intriguing insight of what Bonhoeffer's ethics look like when spelled out in relation to a concrete question. In 'What is meant by "Telling the Truth"?' Bonhoeffer returns to how being good is worked out within social relationships – a theme at the heart of his thinking about the warrant for ethical discourse and his mandates theology. Within a social relationship, the position and role one has bears strongly on one's moral responsibility. Take telling the truth: Kant famously argued that one should always tell the truth in every circumstance, even if one's questioner is a murderer asking the location of a friend in order to kill him. For Bonhoeffer, however, '[T]he truthfulness of a child towards his parents is essentially different from that of the parents towards their child' (*E* 326). He understood that 'the more complex the actual situations of a man's life, the more responsible and the more difficult will be his task of "telling the truth"' (E 327). The point surely is that telling the truth can be used for evil purposes: propaganda does this when it uses accurate facts or genuine information, but uses it with the ultimate objective of dissimulation and deception. As an example, Bonhoeffer imagines a child who is asked by his teacher in front of his class whether it is true that his father often comes home drunk. Though his father may indeed frequently come home drunk, Bonhoeffer argues that because the child has a moral obligation to honour his father, he is justified in answering the question with a 'no' though this is literally untrue. Though the child has lied, in Bonhoeffer's view, he has acted truthfully in a deeper sense. A family (one of Bonhoeffer's divine mandates) has a right to its secrets. The essay, written during or shortly before Bonhoeffer's interrogation, develops a moral justification for the lies Bonhoeffer was telling in service of the truth of the anti-Nazi conspiracy. Telling the truth is not always a simple matter of accurately reporting facts; it demands that we discern the truth that lies beyond literal accuracy.

Towards an ethics of responsible action

Bonhoeffer rejected the Kantian idea that there are timeless moral laws that all people must obey. One immediate consequence might be a feeling of moral vertigo, a sense that without the barrier of timeless moral laws, there is nothing to stop one falling off the edge into a downward spin towards moral chaos. But for Bonhoeffer Christian ethics meant taking responsibility away from the moral rule book and giving it back to the believer (who had 'lost' this responsibility at the Fall). 'The structure of responsible life', Bonhoeffer wrote, 'is conditioned by two factors; life is bound to man and to God and a man's own life is free' (E 194). This sentence could be a summary of this whole book. A responsible ethical life is neither one slavishly bound up in divine law or command, nor to ecclesiastical authority, nor to the verbally inspired text of the Bible. Neither is a responsible ethical life one in which choices are unlimited, nor the moral life unbounded or untrammelled – in short 'free' in the sense that it has not duties or obligations. True responsibility means freedom, and true freedom means responsibility.

Moral responsibility demands more from the Christian than unthinking conformation to moral rules. In Bonhoeffer's ethics, conformation is to a living person through whom God's command comes fresh to each individual each day. This does not mean that what God wills changes from day to day, since God is constant in character and will. In this sense, Bonhoeffer's ethics are not occasionalistic, that is *ad hoc* or once off. But it does mean that Christians take responsibility for discerning the right thing to do, and also for doing it. It means that though God is responsible for the world – and takes responsibility visibly in the cross – Christians take a penultimate responsibility for who they are and what they do. Ultimately, God judges Christians' actions and if they have acted wrongly, they trust in the forgiveness of God, not as a right, but as a promise made by God in Christ. Bonhoeffer welcomed this kind of moral responsibility as a coming of age.

Notes

1   Alasdair MacIntyre's diagnosis of a Western moral crisis points to the Enlightenment as the period in which the Western moral consensus fractured. His *After Virtue*, 2nd edition, Duckworth, 1985, is essential reading for anyone keen to understand contemporary ethics.

2   English translation, 1955.

3   Letter to Eberhard Bethge 27 November 1940.

4   It would be misleading to characterize Bonhoeffer's approach here – a premiss in favour of bodily life, but allowing exceptions – as a form of 'situation ethics'. Situation ethics in its most popular form (Joseph Fletcher) seeks a third way between strict adherence to moral laws and complete freedom by considering the situation and the consequences of moral acts in the light of a few key moral principles, such as love. The difference between situation ethics and Bonhoeffer's ethics may be grasped when we recall the force of his rejection of the idea that in ethics the subject 'works out' the right thing to do for herself. Situation ethics are

precisely the kind of ethics Bonhoeffer imagines arising from the Fall: a human enquiry into right and wrong.

5   See 'Polyphonic Living: Dietrich Bonhoeffer' in *Self and Salvation: Being Transformed*, CUP, 1999, pp. 241–65.

6   See chapter 6 'Method' in *Dietrich Bonhoeffer: His Significance for North Americans*, Larry Rasmussen, Fortress, 1990, pp. 89–110.

7   See *New Studies in Bonhoeffer's 'Ethics'*, Ed. William J. Peck, Edwin Mellen Press, 1987, pp. 59–60.

8   *CD III/4* p. 22.

8

Ethics and the 'world come of age'

From the window of Dietrich Bonhoeffer's cell in 1944 the world cannot have seemed very adult. Barred and set high in the brick wall of his cell, Bonhoeffer's window looked out onto a city crushed from above by Allied bombs and poisoned from within by a decade of Nazi misrule. In neighbouring cells he could hear grown men crying like children. Guards acted like schoolyard bullies. The innocent died and the guilty went free: a world gone mad, not a world grown up. Whatever else it was, Bonhoeffer's prison theology was not a round of applause for the moral maturity of the world.

Neither was it a lamentation. In the first year of his imprisonment, before evidence emerged linking him to the plot to assassinate Hitler, Bonhoeffer expended his energy on preparing for his trial, which he expected would result in his release. When the trial failed to materialize, and when the assassination plot failed in July 1944, Bonhoeffer understood the implications for himself and his relatives, friends and colleagues in the conspiracy. Certainly, Bonhoeffer believed that God

... knows ten thousand ways
To save us from death's door (*LPP* 306)

but it seemed very probable that before long evidence would emerge incriminating him and he knew the wise course was to prepare for the worst scenario. Many men and women would have despaired; Bonhoeffer resumed theology in earnest. Bonhoeffer's smuggled letters to Eberhard Bethge were his last chance to sketch out his new ideas. From April 1944 until he was taken from the relative safety of Tegel Military Interrogation Prison to the Gestapo prison in Prinz-Albrecht-Strasse in October 1944 Bonhoeffer wrote with extraordinary diligence and energy. His theology was critical, to be sure, but oriented to the future and characterized by a profound optimism for theology, the Church, and humanity.

If Bonhoeffer's prison letters mark a new development in his theology, as is widely assumed, do they also suggest a new development in Bonhoeffer's theological ethics? What might ethics be like in a 'world come of age', in which we live 'as if God were not given'? What might a non-religious Christian ethic be like? What might it mean to live out the Gospel as a practice of 'arcane discipline'? The chapter falls into two parts: the first reports the key theological elements of Bonhoeffer's letters to Eberhard Bethge in this last and fruitful year[1] and the second explores the potential of Bonhoeffer's insights for his theological ethics.

Bonhoeffer's prison theology

Bonhoeffer's letter to Bethge of 30 April 1944 sets the agenda for the theological investigation that would occupy him until October. Reflecting expressly on the Western Christianity of which he was a product and a representative, Bonhoeffer asks: '[W]hat is bothering me incessantly is the question what Christianity really is, or indeed who Christ really is, for us today' (*LPP* 279). Unrecognized by many in the Church, a fundamental change has taken place in the orientation of the Western world. The time when people would accept what they were told theologically or religiously is past, and so is the time when people were preoccupied by their own inner life or by the working of their own conscience. Many generations were truly dependent on orthodox religion, with its emphasis on piety and good conscience; but people in the West are now 'moving towards a completely religionless time' (*LPP* 279). People cannot and will not go on practising religion as they have for centuries. For the Church, this new situation will take some getting used to, because its whole nineteen hundred year history has presupposed that people are naturally inclined towards religion; that is the Church's preaching rests upon an assumption of a religious *a priori* of humankind.

What, Bonhoeffer asks, if one day soon, it becomes clear that humankind's religious *a priori* was a 'historically conditioned and transient form of human self-expression' (*LPP* 280) – which was indeed virtually the case, in Bonhoeffer's view, in 1944 – would the disappearance of the illusory religious *a priori* mean that the foundation on which Christianity had been built had been pulled away? Should the few Christians who remained in such a cultural situation be characterized as intellectually dishonest, or as a chosen remnant? And if religious presuppositions really only ever were an 'outer garment' for Christianity, then what is to follow its disappearance ... a religionless Christianity? But what would a religionless Christianity be like?

Bonhoeffer believed his theological questions raised the possibility not only of a new departure for his own theology, but of a new theology that broke the mould of the liberal versus neo-orthodox debate that was characteristic of his era. Bonhoeffer acknowledged that Karl Barth had 'started out along this line of thought, but did not carry it to completion' (*LPP* 280). According to Bonhoeffer, Barth had recognized well enough that the religious outer form of Western Christianity had been slowly peeling away, but instead of embracing this change he had tried to restore humankind's religious *a priori*.[2] Instead of a 'restoration' of religion, Bonhoeffer sets out the stall of his theological project with several very practical questions, including what 'do a church, a community, a sermon, a liturgy, a Christian life mean in a religionless world? How do we speak of God – without religion, i.e. without the temporally conditioned presuppositions of metaphysics, inwardness and so on?' (*LPP* 280). Crucially, Bonhoeffer adds, in

> what way are we 'religionless-secular' Christians, in what way are we the *ecclesia*,[3] those who are called forth, not regarding ourselves from a religious point of view as specially favoured, but rather as belonging wholly to the world?

More positively, '[d]oes the secret discipline, or alternatively the difference ... between the penultimate and the ultimate, take on new importance here?' (*LPP* 280–1). That is, will Christians need to find new, arcane ways of being present in the penultimate reality of this world in which they keep ultimate things to themselves not out of shame or doubt, but as an act of kindness to the penultimate? Paul had challenged the 'religious' presuppositions of the Apostles in Jerusalem by asking whether circumcision really is a condition of justification. Have the outward trappings of religion the contemporary equivalents of Gentile circumcision?

There is a curious personal motivation, Bonhoeffer writes, for his questions: as a Christian he often feels more drawn to religionless people than to the religious, not with evangelistic or apologetic intent, but because he feels more instinctively in fellowship with them. With the religionless, he feels able calmly and naturally to speak God's name. But religious people bring God up like a *deus ex machina* – a divine theatrical device dropped into the action of a play to resolve its plot. God functions for them either as a solution of apparently insoluble problems, or as a means of exploiting moments of human need and weakness. But, Bonhoeffer concludes, 'I should like to speak of God not on the boundaries but at the centre, not in weakness but in strength; and therefore not in death and guilt but in man's life and goodness' (*LPP 282*).

On 5 May, Bonhoeffer took up again the theme of his letter from a few days earlier. Rudolf Bultmann's 1941 essay 'New Testament and Mythology' had been widely debated since its publication, not least within the Confessing Church, which was trying to find a theological identity beyond the neo-orthodoxy of Karl Barth, its erstwhile leading light. Bultmann had proposed that certain New Testament concepts, such as miracle and ascension, needed to be 'demythologized', that is stripped of their metaphysical, unhistorical and unreal outer form. Bonhoeffer admired Bultmann's essay for the same reason he admired Barth: Bultmann at least recognized that Christianity faced a credibility problem. But Bultmann was essentially a liberal at heart who, like all theological liberals before him, tried to make the gospel more palatable by hacking off its sharper edges. For Bonhoeffer, 'you can't, as Bultmann supposes, separate God and miracle, but you must be able to interpret and proclaim *both* in a "non-religious" sense' (*LPP* 285). In this respect Bultmann had not gone too far; he had not gone far enough!

Interpreting Christian faith and theology religiously means to speak metaphysically and individualistically, neither of which is particularly biblical. The Old Testament shows no interest at all in the question of saving one's soul, but keeps focused on this-worldly righteousness and the Kingdom of God. Even Paul's idea of being justified by grace – the cornerstone of Reformation theology – is not chiefly concerned with the salvation of the individual, but with the extent of God's righteousness. In sum, what Bonhoeffer means is that what 'is above this world is, in the gospel, intended to exist *for* this world' (*LPP* 286), not in the sense that humanity becomes the centre of attention, but in the sense that the key doctrines of creation, incarnation, crucifixion and resurrection are all *this-worldly* in orientation. Barth's approach to these theological challenges amounts, Bonhoeffer believes, to a 'positivism of revelation' in which Christian doctrines such as the virgin birth, the Trinity, etc., are all thought of as equally important, and which must be accepted as a whole or not at all. The result is that the Church stands where religion once stood – not altogether a bad thing – but the Church, though 'pure' is isolated from the world, which is left to its own devices.

On 20 May, Bonhoeffer again took up his theological investigation. He now began to air a musical metaphor for the non-religious Christianity he was reaching towards:

> ... God wants us to love him eternally with our whole hearts – not in such a way as to injure or weaken our earthly love, but to provide a kind of *cantus firmus* [i.e. the central tune around which a piece of music is built] to which other melodies of life provide the counterpoint. One of these contrapuntal themes (which have their own complete independence but are yet related to the *cantus firmus*) is earthly affection. (*LPP* 303)

Good polyphonic music is like a life which has Christ as its central melody, and in which other themes and harmonies are free from time to time to come into their own, but which always come back to their basic task of adding to and complementing the *cantus firmus*. It was over a month before Bonhoeffer returns to this insight. Watching his fellow prisoners, Bonhoeffer is struck by how shallow they are, how dependent their moods are on the meal before them, or the air raid they are in. 'By contrast, Christianity puts us into many different dimensions of life at the same time; we make room in ourselves, to some extent, for God and the whole world' (*LPP* 310). By holding joy and suffering, personal anxiety and broader perspective together, Christian life is able to remain multidimensional and polyphonic. In the same letter, Bonhoeffer reports the outcome of recently reading a book on the world-view of physics. 'It has brought home to me quite clearly how wrong it is to use God as a stop-gap for the incompleteness of our knowledge' (*LPP* 311). This is true of the borders between 'religion' and science, where the more we know about the natural world the less God is needed as an explanation for natural, scientific processes and problems. But the same is increasingly true of other areas of human life, such as death and suffering and guilt, which people are much more willing to deal with without recourse to God. If he is right, then God has not been 'pushed out' from spheres of influence that once belonged to God, God never properly belonged at the outer edges of human knowledge:

> God is no stop-gap; he must be recognized at the centre of life, not when we are at the end of our resources; it is his will to be recognized in life, and not only when death comes; in health and vigour, and not only in our suffering; in our activities, and not only in sin. (*LPP* 312)

When did the movement towards the autonomy of humankind begin – when, that is, did Western culture discover the laws beyond God's law by which to live scientifically, socially, politically, aesthetically and ethically? In each of these areas, Bonhoeffer continued on 8 June (two days after the Allied invasion of Normandy), beginning in the thirteenth century human beings have learnt to manage 'without recourse to the "working hypothesis" called "God" (*LPP* 325). In science and ethics the assumption that one can cope without God is so commonplace it is hardly remarked. But from the middle of the eighteenth century, this has been increasingly true of 'religious' questions. Both Protestants and Catholics have tended to react to these developments as if they are essentially anti-Christian. Christian apologetics has tried to prove to the world that it cannot, after all, live confidently without God, and tried even more vainly to keep the world from encroaching further into any remaining religious spheres of influence, such as guilt and death. For Bonhoeffer, this kind of Christian apologetics is pointless, ignoble and unchristian. It is pointless 'because it seems to me like an attempt to put a grown-up man back into adolescence, i.e. to make him dependent on things on which he is, in fact, no longer dependent' (*LPP* 327). It is ignoble because it attempts to exploit people's weaknesses without their consent. Finally it is unchristian because it confuses one historical form of the Christian religion with the way human beings must always be in relation to Christ.

On 27 June, Bonhoeffer reopened the question of the significance of the Old Testament as the lens through which the New Testament must be read. The faith of the Old Testament is not, he asserts, a faith based on the human thirst for redemption – or rather, in the Old Testament, redemption is conceived in this-worldly rather than other-worldly terms. The redemption God gives the Israelites is not the promise of life after death, but liberation from slavery in Egypt or from exile in Babylon. Redemption is something that takes place in history. The religion of the Jews was thus in sharp contrast with other Eastern religions, which tended to contain myths of redemption beyond the grave. Christianity has always, to be sure, been a religion of redemption. However, the Church has been mistaken in abandoning the this-worldly religion of the Jews in favour of other-worldly redemption theologies. It is understandable, and even to an extent appropriate, that this should be so, since Christianity proclaims the hope of the resurrection, which is genuinely a promise of redemption. But even this redemption is misinterpreted if it is thought to mean 'redemption from cares, distress, fears, and longings, from sin and death, in a better world beyond the grave ... The Christian, unlike the devotees of the redemption myths, has no last line of escape available from earthly tasks and difficulties into the eternal, but, like Christ himself ... he must drink the earthly cup to the dregs' (*LPP* 336–7).

Three days later Bonhoeffer resumed his line of thought. It is not only Christianity that has held the world back from its maturity: existentialism and psychotherapy – which are but secularized offshoots of Christian religion – feed off human need and despair. But when one looks at Jesus, he was concerned only with calling people away from their sin. He did not first require a sinner to dwell introspectively and guiltily on her sin, but to turn away from it to the kingdom of God. A few days later Bonhoeffer was aspiring to a 'non-religious interpretation of biblical concepts'. With God pushed out at the extremes, religious people became increasingly preoc-cupied by the 'personal', the 'private' and the 'inner': the hunting ground of modern pastoral workers had contracted to the secret areas of a person's life known to a man's valet! In this, pastoral workers resemble nothing so much as tabloid journalists grubbing about in the dustbins of a man's life in the hope of finding some juicy secret on which to seize. Of course men and women are sinful. But such clerical sniffing out of sins mistakenly supposes that someone can be addressed as a sinner only when his weaknesses have been exposed. It also erroneously supposes that the private and inner life of a man or woman is who he or she essentially is. In fact, the inner life is only one of many things that matter: to put it crudely, was Napoleon wicked because he committed adultery, or because his hubris condemned Europe to bitter war for a generation? What Bonhoeffer wants is therefore:

[T]o start from the premise that God shouldn't be smuggled into some last secret place, but that we should frankly recognize that the world, and people, have come of age, that we shouldn't run man down in his worldliness, but confront him with God at his strongest point.... (*LPP* 346)

On 16 July, Bonhoeffer turned again to history. His reading in prison was heavily weighted towards history and the reading was paying off. Human autonomy in theology came about with Lord Herbert of Cherbury's thesis that reason alone (without revelation) was a sufficient basis for religious knowledge. In ethics, it occurred when Montaigne and Bodin substituted rules of life for the commandments. Machiavelli likewise expediently replaced political morality with 'reasons of state'. Grotius underpinned the autonomy of human society by setting up natural law as international law, which is valid '*etsi deus non daretur*', that is, as if there were no God. Neither is it only human beings that live 'as if there were no God': the universe too appears self-subsisting. Bonhoeffer concludes with some drama that:

> we cannot be honest unless we recognize that we have to live in the world *etsi deus non daretur*. And this is just what we do recognize – before God! God would have us know that we must live as men who manage our lives without him. The God who is with us is the God who forsakes us. (*LPP* 360)

This is the culmination of the argument and the high water mark of Bonhoeffer's theology, the moment at which Bonhoeffer's new thinking concerning the 'world come of age' and 'religionless Christianity' is brought together with his christology.

> Before God and with God we live without God. God lets himself be pushed out of the world on to the cross. He is weak and powerless in the world, and that is precisely the way, the only way, in which he is with us and helps us. Matthew 8:17 [he 'took our infirmities and bore our diseases'] makes it quite clear that Christ helps us, not by virtue of his omnipotence, but by virtue of his weakness and suffering. (*LPP* 360–1)

This is the decisive difference between true Christians and all other religious believers: religion looks in human distress to the power of God in the world, but the 'Bible directs man to God's powerlessness and suffering; *only the suffering God can help*' (*LPP* 361, my emphasis).

This defining moment in his theology came days before the attempt on Hitler's life. The day after the attempt, when it was perfectly obvious the coup had failed, Bonhoeffer was again pursuing his theme, and writing of his *Discipleship* as an attempt to live a holy life. On 28 July Bonhoeffer summarizes what he has said about the differences between the Old and the New Testaments: in the Old the blessing includes the cross, and in the New the cross includes the blessing. Days later he adds that the Church must come out of stagnation and tackle these questions in open dialogue with the world. He makes a start at this dialogue in an outline for a short book summarizing the themes he has developed in correspondence with Bethge. The planned book was to have three chapters. In the first, he intended to offer a stock-take of Christianity in which he would detail the 'coming of age' of humankind, human religiouslessness, and the woebegone attempts of Protestantism to defend itself against the process. He planned a section on public morals as a detailed exploration of his theses, and in particular sexual behaviour. In the second chapter he planned to offer the positive part of his argument, a necessary follow on from the critical note of his first chapter. In this, he would rework his christology, so that Jesus would be visible as 'the man for others', the Crucified man who lives from the transcendent. A non-religious interpretation of biblical concepts, such as creation, atonement, faith and the last things, was to follow. It helps greatly that the non-religious interpretation was to flow from his realization of Jesus as the man for others who lives out of the transcendent, for it affords us a glimpse of how he might have interpreted biblical concepts in ways that they became available to serve human beings; deriving them from the transcendent, but transforming their purpose. In a third chapter he anticipated setting out his conclusions for the Church, which, in the pattern of the man for others, 'is the church only when it exists for others' (*LPP* 382). The Church should sell its property and make the resources available to those in need. Clergy should either earn their keep in secular employment or live off free-will offerings (rather than be paid, then as now for most German churches, as civil servants with funds gathered through the state tax system). A revision of Christian apologetics is long overdue, he writes, as well as reform of training for ministry and the pattern of clerical life. Bonhoeffer returned only briefly and in passing to his theological reflections in the surviving correspondence. He wrote throughout August and September to Bethge, but the letters were lost, and the correspondence halted when Bonhoeffer was removed from Tegel prison.

Ethics and the 'world come of age'

Tegel prison was not the best place to think through a new theology, and wartime Berlin was not the best moment in which to be doing it. Josef Goebbels, the Nazi Propaganda Minister, had ordered prison libraries purged of any book that might subvert the war effort. Even with his parents on the look-out for books on his behalf, Bonhoeffer did not have all the reading matter he wanted or needed to develop his ideas to their fullest potential. And as he wrote winsomely to his friend, 'it is harder to think without an echo'. Bonhoeffer tried his utmost not to put any pressure on Bethge, but it was impossible for him to keep pace. The letters were the main focus of Bonhoeffer's attention: for Bethge they competed with his new wife, baptismal preparations, avoiding Allied bombers on journeys to and from his *Wehrmacht* unit and the numbing boredom of his day-to-day soldier's life. Yet Bethge was a capable theologian and in one reply, he identified an important problem raised by Bonhoeffer's peregrinations. Responding to Bonhoeffer's thoughts on the ways a Christian theology of redemption tends to flee the day-to-day life into the promise of life after death, Bethge replies, 'It seems to me unbiblical to regard eschatology as an evasion' (*LPP* 356). It is a very acute remark. It is certainly true that the Bible directs us to God's weakness and suffering. It is equally true that this insight has been misunderstood, neglected and distorted for the greater part of Christian history. But it is not true that this is *all* the Bible directs us to: the ultimate end-point of the New Testament is a City of Gold. It is not correct to interpret Bonhoeffer's prison theology as suggesting that redemption *only* takes place this side of the grave, simply that truly grasping what this ultimate otherworldly redemption means should send the Christian back to this world in renewed commitment to serving others. He did not doubt the resurrection as some critics have malignly suggested (as he went to his death he said 'this is the end – for me the beginning of life'). Yet the senses in which a fuller realization of a theology of the last things could contribute to sending his readers back to the world are limited in these letters. Neither does Bonhoeffer make the mistake, typical of many theologies of the suffering God, of equating the weakness of Christ and the powerlessness of God with a divine inability to make any difference. Bonhoeffer's deep conviction is that it is *through* weakness, suffering and power *that* God is with us and helps us. Being 'pushed out' onto the cross, God is not reduced to absenteeism, but helps us by virtue of his weakness. The silence on the cross is not craven, hopeless or helpless because through it Christ 'wins power and space in the world by his weakness' (*LPP* 361).

And what of ethics? If there is a religionless interpretation of biblical concepts, a religionless Christianity, are there also to be 'religionless ethics'? Bonhoeffer's theological correspondence with Bethge mentions ethics in passing as one of the historical instances of a growth in human autonomy. And though in his outline for a book, Bonhoeffer had hoped to dedicate a section to public sexual morality as an example of Protestantism's misguided attempt to defend itself, the references are few and brief. There are two possibilities. The first is that the prison theology follows in the wake of a religionless ethics already developed by Bonhoeffer in the book he was writing during the war. If this is right, then the *Ethics* already are a 'religionless ethics'. Does Bonhoeffer's *Ethics* already offer us a choice between religious ethics (i.e. ethics after the Fall) and non-religious ethics (i.e. ethics beyond good and evil)?

The second possibility is that in prison Bonhoeffer's theological ethics take a significant shift in direction. Bonhoeffer does not say he has become cautious about his *Ethics*, in the way he does about *Discipleship*. There are considerable signs of continuity between the theology of the prison letters and his earlier theology. Yet in my view the letters *do* suggest a significant shift in at least one respect that concerns ethics.

Very nearly all of Bonhoeffer's ethics prior to April 1944 are premised on the idea that Christian ethics are distinct from all other ethics and constitute a critique of all other ethics. 'Very nearly all' because it is unwise to be categorical; but also because in his mandates theology, Bonhoeffer was already experimenting (without complete success) with crediting the world with some kind of moral autonomy, as well as with the categories of 'ultimate' and 'penultimate' that resurface in his 'world come of age'. Nevertheless, it is certainly true that the greater part of his theological effort in ethics before April 1944 was dedicated to spelling out the implication of the Fall, which was that the human ability to decide between right and wrong, good and evil, resulted from the Fall and marked a sustained human disobedience of God. In *Discipleship* Bonhoeffer attempted, in a manner he did not revoke but came to see the weakness of, to carve out a space for the Church in the world. In *Ethics* he gave up this kind of two-spheres thinking to oscillate, creatively and dangerously, between reiterating the distinctiveness of Christian ethics and stating afresh a commitment to the presence of Christ in the natural and in the mandates.

So far Bonhoeffer had thought through the ethics of the conspiracy for his friends, but the moment had to come when he sought to grasp the faith of the church in general in its relationship to this secular world – a world that his own family history had made him close to. (*DB* 857)

The question that the prison theology raises is whether Bonhoeffer's hope that the Church should resist smuggling God into the world and instead 'should frankly recognize that the world, and people, have come of age, that we shouldn't run man down in his worldliness, but confront him with God at his strongest point ...' (*LPP* 346) would require a rethinking of his whole insistence on the distinctiveness of Christian ethics. If the sharp distinction between Christian and non-Christian ethics were to be abandoned, would Bonhoeffer's acute and unflinching critique of contemporary immorality and weak and lazy ethics be lost with it? Bonhoeffer gives one indication of a direction in which an answer might be developed when he asks if religionless Christianity might mean developing the idea of an arcane discipline – a way of being in the penultimate 'as if God were not there' without ever losing sight of Jesus Christ. In his earlier theology Bonhoeffer had worked to express how Jesus is Lord of the Church. With the phrase 'Jesus the man for others', he expressed Jesus' Lordship over the religionless too. Yet finally, the brute truth is that though he was aware of the question of the ethical implications of his prison theology, and recognized its importance, he did not work out the implications of the 'world come of age' for ethics – at least not in writing. But this is not a tragedy. Bonhoeffer had already done enough to make clear that a Christian must take responsibility for her own moral views and actions and not hide behind those of a moral guru. Making sense of ethics in a world come of age is up to us.

Notes

1   Three books give indispensable guidance for reading Bonhoeffer's prison letters: Eberhard Bethge's *Dietrich Bonhoeffer: A Biography*, Fortress, 2000, chapter 13; Clifford J. Green's *Bonhoeffer: A Theology of Sociality*, revised edition, Eerdmans, 1999, chapter 6; and Ralph K. Wüstenberg's *A Theology of Life: Dietrich Bonhoeffer's Religionless Christianity*, Eerdmans, 1998.

2   This was an accusation Karl Barth rejected, though chiefly and disingenuously because he thought Bonhoeffer didn't know or understand his theology well enough.

3   I.e. the Church. In the original Greek, *ecclesia* invites the word-play Bonhoeffer now uses.

9

'Are we still of any use?'

Is Dietrich Bonhoeffer an antique figure whose experience and perspective is so remote that his voice fails to carry from his time to our own? This is an uncomfortable question to ask. Bonhoeffer was courageous, intelligent; loyal to friends and family and, in the darkest moment of German history, he was on the side of the Angels. Yet these qualities have no necessary bearing on the value of his politics, theology or ethics today. Any theologian, any thinker from the past, serves us best when we resist the urge to domesticate them by our approval and admiration. Outstanding Christian thinkers are those who retain the capacity to shock us by the truth of their insights as we read our own dilemmas in the harsh light of their 'otherness'. Bonhoeffer's theology and ethics have this classic quality but their potential is only realized when we resist the urge to tame his legacy by assuming that it is easily applied to our own situation. In this final chapter, I want therefore to pose three critical questions to Bonhoeffer's legacy.

'After Ten Years'

Shortly before his arrest, Bonhoeffer wrote an essay titled 'After Ten Years: A Reckoning made at New Year 1943' (*LPP* 3–17). The essay was a gift for the handful of co-conspirators closest to him with whom he had shared a decade of anti-Nazi resistance. The tone of the essay is one of gratitude for lessons learned in the struggle, but it confronts hard questions about the moral consequences of conspiracy. 'The great masquerade of evil has played havoc with all our ethical concepts', Bonhoeffer writes:

> For evil to appear disguised as light, charity, historical necessity, or social justice is quite bewildering to anyone brought up on our traditional ethical concepts, while for the Christian who bases his life on the Bible, it merely confirms the fundamental wickedness of evil. (*LPP* 4)

For Bonhoeffer, the evils of Nazism had shown up the flaws in six types of moral character. Reasonable people thought that with a little reason they could bend the Nazis into a more morally acceptable position. Moral fanatics thought that by unbending adherence to their moral principles they could battle the evils of Nazism. Some contented themselves with a salved rather than a clear conscience without realizing that a bad conscience may be stronger and more wholesome than a deluded one. Others obeyed orders, as if doing one's duty exhausted one's responsibility. Those who asserted their own freedom were prepared to compromise truth and assent to what is bad in order to avoid something worse. Finally there were women and men who treasured their own private virtue who were prepared to avoid taking responsibility if it means incurring personal guilt, even if this means turning a blind eye to injustice. The moral types Bonhoeffer sketches represent recognizable caricatures of philosophical ethics: utilitarians and pragmatists, socialists, Protestants, Kantians, existentialists, Pharisees. Even if we acknowledge that these caricatures were drawn before his groundbreaking prison letters, there is no reason to think Bonhoeffer subsequently demurred from the powerful and succinct dismissal of non-Christian ethics expressed at this point. None of these forms of ethics, he asserts, have proved sufficient to meet the demands that Nazi Germany has made of them. So who is able to confront the situation? Only the person

> whose final standard is not his reason, his principles, his conscience, his freedom, or his virtue, but who is ready to sacrifice all this when he is called to obedient and responsible action in faith and in exclusive allegiance to God – the responsible person, who tries to make his whole life an answer to the question and call of God. (*LPP* 5) [translation amended]

Bonhoeffer accepted that the reasons behind collusion of most Germans in Nazi policy and practice were complex. They had little to do with fear – too many Germans fought bravely in the Nazi cause for that casual explanation to be sustainable. Rather, the explanation lay in the deep-rooted German tradition of uncritical obedience to authority. For Bonhoeffer, God's demand for responsible human 'action in a bold venture of faith' is in the sharpest possible contrast to blind obedience. Obeying God calls for complete obedience, yet not blind obedience, for it involves both discernment and responsibility. Anyone willing to take such responsibility must be willing to incur personal guilt and thereby to rely ultimately not on their own strength or goodness but upon God's forgiveness and consolation.

Bonhoeffer's point is morally shocking: the conspiracy was sinful and the conspirators were cast upon the mercy of God. Bonhoeffer seems to suggest that assassinating Hitler and thereby curtailing Nazi rule is morally reprehensible. If true, would this condemnation also apply to the Allied servicemen and women engaged in the war? The question is legitimate: Bonhoeffer had never expressly revoked his pre-war view that war is wrong and the logic of his position is that combatants, just like conspirators, are thrust upon God's mercy since war can never be in keeping with God's purposes. Yet in the essay Bonhoeffer confines himself specifically to the moral cost of conspiracy:

> We have been silent witnesses of evil deeds; we have been drenched by many storms; we have learnt the arts of equivocation and pretence; experience has made us suspicious of others and kept us from being truthful and open; intolerable conflicts have worn us down and even made us cynical. (*LPP* 16)

Most of us will thankfully never face similar moral circumstances. The conspiracy was, Bonhoeffer understood, an emergency situation; what we might now more casually call a 'moral grey area'. In such borderline areas the true nature of human ethics is brought to light together with the need to re-evaluate and reshape them. In 1933 Bonhoeffer had spoken critically, in his radio address on the 'Führer principle', of the cult of success. Without abandoning his suspicion of the Nazi cult of success, 'after ten years' Bonhoeffer now recognized that the moral significance of success could not easily be ignored:

> Although it is certainly not true that success justifies an evil deed and shady means, it is impossible to regard success as something that is ethically quite neutral. The fact is that historical success

creates a basis for the continuance of life, and it is still a moot point whether it is ethically more responsible to take the field like a Don Quixote against a new age, or to admit one's defeat, accept the new age, and agree to serve it. In the last resort success makes history; and the ruler of history repeatedly brings good out of evil over the heads of the history-makers. Simply to ignore the ethical significance of success is a short circuit created by dogmatists who think unhistorically and irresponsibly; and it is good for us sometimes to be compelled to grapple seriously with the ethical problem of success. As long as goodness is successful, we can afford the luxury of regarding it as having no ethical significance; it is when success is achieved by evil means that the problem arises. (LPP 6–7)

In 1943, though the Confessing Church had failed, Bonhoeffer still hoped the conspiracy would succeed. But he recognized that its success, if it came, would be by evil means: lying, treason and murder. Could those who had resorted to such means still play a role in the reconstruction of a post-Nazi Germany? His final question is therefore not merely rhetorical: 'Are we still of any use? What we shall need is not geniuses, or cynics, or misanthropes, or clever tacticians, but plain, honest, straightforward men [and women]' (*LPP* 16–17) [translation amended].

This question – 'are we still of any use?' – can help to form a structure in which to evaluate Bonhoeffer's politics, theology and ethics, as well as for reading our own situation in the light of his legacy.

Are we of political use?

In the 1930s and 1940s the future of democracy was far from certain. After the First World War political democracies had replaced autocratic monarchies in many European nations, but in all but a handful of countries they had proved weak and incapable. During the second half of Bonhoeffer's life most Europeans lived under dictatorships of Nazi, Fascist or Communist hue. The 'triumph' of democracy in twentieth-century Europe is therefore 'a story of narrow squeaks and unexpected twists, not inevitable victories and forward marches'.[1] To take the view, as Bonhoeffer and his co-conspirators did, that Germany was not yet suited to democratic government was not, therefore, unreasonable. For Bonhoeffer, Nazism was bad because it transgressed the law, ruled barbarously and had taken Germany (and Europe) into the chaos of total war. He was not troubled by the Nazis' lack of a democratic mandate; on the contrary, he was suspicious of the Führer's popularity; for though the Leader misled the people the people were willing to be misled. Bonhoeffer's view of the need for 'legitimate' political authority is implicit in his lectures on *Creation and Fall* and spelled out theologically in his concept of the divine mandates within his *Ethics*. A recently uncovered letter makes them plainer still. Writing to Paul Lehmann in 1941 Bonhoeffer asks himself about the political future of Germany:

> Nothing would be worse than to impose upon her any Anglo-Saxon form of government – as much as I should like it. It simply would not work ... As far as I know Germany, it will just be impossible, for instance, to restore complete freedom of speech, of press, of association. That sort of thing would throw Germany right into the same abyss. I think we must try to find a Germany in which justice, lawfulness, freedom of the churches is being restored. I hope there will [be] something like an authoritarian *Rechtsstaat* as the Germans call it. It will need a long process of education before the people as a whole will be in a position to enjoy all the liberties it used to have.[2]

Bonhoeffer envisaged for Germany a postwar political system not unlike that depicted in Thomas More's *Utopia* (1516) in which an educated élite constituted a ruling class; an aristocracy not of bloodlines, but of virtue and education, would rule not for their own benefit, but in the interest of the common good. The theological basis of Bonhoeffer's politics was grounded in his reworking of the Lutheran idea that those in authority were mandated with an office, in which power was bounded by law; jurisdiction by duty and responsibility. He gives a good example of this in his wedding sermon for Eberhard Bethge and Renate Bonhoeffer, written from his prison cell in 1943. Working out from Pauline social teaching he characterized the relation of men and women within marriage:

> Now when the husband is called 'the head of the wife', and it goes on to say 'as Christ is head of the Church' (Ephesians 5:23), something of the divine splendour is reflected in our earthly relationships, and this reflection we should recognize and honour. The dignity that is here ascribed to the man lies, not in any capacities or qualities of his own, but in the office conferred on him by

143

his marriage. The wife should see her husband clothed in this dignity. But for him it is a supreme responsibility. As the head, it is he who is responsible for his wife, for their marriage, and for their home. On him falls the care and protection of the family; he represents it to the outside world; he is its mainstay and comfort; he is the master of the house, who exhorts, punishes, helps, and comforts, and stands for it before God. (*LPP* 45)

There is nothing remarkable about the views in this sermon: most couples in 1943 accepted that a husband was head of the wife. The reason it is striking is that such a view of the office and authority of husband – as of a Pastor, a teacher, a judge or a politician – is now the exception rather than the rule in Western countries. Turning again to politics, Bonhoeffer's views still have modern counterparts. There is no reason why a view common in the past and uncommon now is necessarily wrong: it is a vanity of the present always to assume it is an improvement on the past. But the experience of the past sixty years does make it necessary to question such a view of social and political authority. Can we so glibly use God to under-write the rule by an élite (whether an élite based on gender, education or political purity)? In some contemporary states, such as Singapore or Burma, national leaders maintain that people have not yet reached a level of maturity sufficient for democratic politics. There are, to be sure, hazards in deifying any human political system (and what else could be meant by pledging allegiance to our nation's flag?). Christians have only very recently learned to applaud democracy – some still suspect it.[3] Yet just as relations between men and women have been revolutionized since 1945, so too has our sense of the nature and value of democracy as a basic condition of the accountability of political authority. The moral, economic and political case for asserting that democratic politics constitutes a fundamental condition of human freedom[4] is now overwhelming.

Many commentators pass over Bonhoeffer's political views by applauding Bonhoeffer for taking politics seriously in the context of Lutheranism's tendency to separate faith and politics. In this, they follow Reinhold Niebuhr's eulogy in 1945:

Bonhoeffer, less known than Martin Niemoeller, will become better known. Not only his martyr's death, but also his actions and precepts contain within them the hope of a revitalized Protestant faith in Germany. It will be a faith, religiously more profound than that of many of his critics; but it will have learned to overcome the one fateful error of German Protestantism, the complete dichotomy between faith and political life.[5]

To my mind, passing too hastily over Bonhoeffer's political views is a mistake. Why?

Bonhoeffer's prison letters are generally understood to affirm the maturity of the world. A closer reading suggests that his affirmation of 'a world come of age' applies more readily to a small, educated, Western élite such as his family and co-conspirators: people like him. It may be true, as he wrote in 'After Ten Years', that we 'have for once learned to see the great events of world history from below, from the perspective of the outcast, the suspects, the maltreated, the powerless, the oppressed, the reviled – in short, from the perspective of those who suffer' (*LPP* 17). But in spite of Bonhoeffer's optimistic faith in benevolent autocracy, that perspective can simply become a powerful weapon in the armoury of any ruling élite. Bonhoeffer's failure to see the *good* inherent in the political freedom of democratic politics may well be understandable given his experience of democracy in the Weimar Republic, but this does not mean it can be passed over. Niebuhr was right: Bonhoeffer *did* overcome the dichotomy between faith and political life. Moreover, against the overwhelmingly trivial character of contemporary politics, Bonhoeffer's political thinking is serious. But the disturbing implication of Niebuhr's remark is that if his politics are flawed, his ethics and theology may be flawed too.

Are we of theological use?

Is there enough in Bonhoeffer's writings with which to rebuff Karl Barth's suggestion that systematic theology was not his real strength? Bonhoeffer's most academically thorough theological works were university dissertations submitted when he was very young. In the last ten years of his life he devoted at least as much energy to the Church struggle and opposition to the Nazis as to theology. Even if he had had the time, libraries and scholarly community to resource the kind of systematic theology produced by other twentieth-century German theologians, would he have been inclined to do so? It is certainly the case that Dietrich Bonhoeffer's theology does not have the magisterial structure of Barth's *Church Dogmatics* – what does? It is also true that his circumstances foreclosed the opportunities for dialogue with critics of his theology that would have helped him to sharpen his arguments. Whatever his situation in life it was in any case his style to make bold statements – such as 'only a suffering God can help' – that should properly be held in tension or balance with other theological insights – such as a fully worked theology of hope and last things. Nevertheless Bonhoeffer's theology has more consistency and coherence than it is often credited with and his originality and flare have left a legacy that remains creative when more careful and thoughtful theologies, such as that of his teacher Reinhold Seeberg, have been forgotten.

The consistency in Bonhoeffer's theology arises from his attempt to use the best of liberal theology to critique Karl Barth's dialectical theology, to use the best of Barth's insights to critique liberal theology, and to use the mash created by these processes to ferment a theology that is neither liberal nor neo-orthodox. From 1933, at least, Bonhoeffer's theology was also consistent in being biblically oriented and often explicitly biblically based. The 'post-liberal' or 'post-critical' method of Bonhoeffer's biblical hermeneutics was lifted from Karl Barth, but Bonhoeffer used his borrowed tool with originality, not least in reflecting more consistently and vigorously on the Old Testament as a source for theology than was common then or now. Finally, the christology Bonhoeffer formed in his 1933 lectures constitutes the central light that illuminates many of the political, theological and ethical subjects he attends to. Christ is at the centre of the *Sanctorum Communio*; christology is *the* academic discipline because with christology alone is the one central question of human life asked 'Who is Jesus Christ for you today? *Discipleship* is following Christ's call; in the *Ethics* believers are described as conformed to Christ; and in prison Jesus is the man for others and the presence of God is made visible in the weakness and suffering of the cross. Christ is the *cantus firmus* in the polyphony of Bonhoeffer's theology. Christology is not the only thread to run through the weave of Bonhoeffer's theology, but it helps to show how coherence may be found in his work, even though his style of writing and choice of subject matter varied so greatly.

Are we of ethical use?

Alasdair MacIntyre hypothesizes that:

> in the actual world which we inhabit the language of morality is in ... [a] state of grave disorder ... What we possess, if this view is true, are the fragments of a conceptual scheme, parts which now lack those contexts from which their significance is derived.

We possess indeed simulacra of morality, we continue to use many of the key expressions. But we have – very largely, if not entirely – lost our comprehension, both theoretical and practical, of morality.[6]

In three successive books MacIntyre develops a powerful case for this thesis. He traces the history of moral concepts such as 'virtue' and shows that while the understanding of what particular virtues such as courage, honour or justice have altered from time to time and place to place, throughout much of the past two and a half millennia human societies, though they have differed in what they thought was virtuous, have shared a common sense that virtues mattered. Beginning roughly with the Enlightenment that shared under-standing of morality began to fragment. In particular the common sense on which morality depended for its coherence upon God broke apart. As belief in God declined, the idea developed that human beings do not follow moral laws given by a Divinity who acts still as a moral referee, but that men and women in reality create their own morality.

Dietrich Bonhoeffer (at least until 1944) believed like MacIntyre that contemporary morality is in a parlous condition. But the chaos of contemporary ethics was not, for Bonhoeffer, explained as the loss of a common moral sense – as if until, say the Enlightenment, human ethics were in good shape. For him, all human attempts to be good are to be viewed from the biblical story of the Fall in terms of sin. Today, for anyone outside the Church and even some within it, the concept of 'sin' is considered by turns irrelevant, intolerant, or ridiculous. By and large, Christians only have themselves to blame for this: for decades Christians have trivialized human sin by reducing moral discourse to smug and niggling criticism of human weaknesses. Bonhoeffer was not interested in sniffing out personal sin. His concern was with the ways in which bad deeds arise from being bad. 'In Adam' sin is a way of being as well as a way of acting. To put it crudely, Hitler was not a sinner because he kept a mistress but because he put himself in the place of God. Christian ethics is therefore distinct from all other ethics in that it alone flows out of a restored unity with the will of God. In 1944 Bonhoeffer was possibly moving towards a reconsideration of the relationship of the Christian and the secular ethically as well as theologically, but there is little reason to suppose that such a reappraisal would have involved becoming soft on sin or soft on the causes of sin. Bonhoeffer's understanding of sin addresses three contrasting groups of people. It addresses liberal Christians, who have lost confidence in speaking of sin at all. It addresses evangelicals, who trivialize talk of sin by squinting exclusively at personal sins. And it addresses non-believers by confronting their sin not at their weak points (their sins of weakness) but at their strong points (their sins of strength). Bonhoeffer's injunction to each of these groups is the same: be conformed to Christ.

Bonhoeffer's ethics also take responsibility seriously. Bonhoeffer knew that his decisions and actions could have concrete consequences for himself and for those close to him. In prison he gave up an escape plan because it would jeopardize his family (*DB* 826–8). He was aware too that his involvement with the conspiracy would compromise the Church; when it comes to treason a Lutheran Pastor cannot act as a private individual. He could not resign his position in the Confessing Church during the war without damaging the conspiracy, but he accepted he would have to resign the Pastorate at the end of the war rather than implicate the Church in his morally controversial actions. In this recognition there was no trace of bitterness or regret towards the Church, the conspiracy, or to the events in which his life had been caught up:

> Now I want to assure you that I haven't for a moment regretted coming back in 1939 – nor any of the consequences either. I knew quite well what I was doing, and I acted with a clear conscience. I've no wish to cross out of my life anything that has happened since, either to me personally ... or as regards events in general. And I regard my being kept here [in prison] ... as being involved in Germany's fate, as I was resolved to be. (*LPP* 174)

Because of this, and in keeping with the Bonhoeffer family *sang-froid*, he resisted casting his imprisonment in a heroic light:

> When people suggest ... that I'm 'suffering' here, I reject the thought. It seems to me a profanation. These things mustn't be dramatized ... Of course, a great deal here is horrible, but where isn't? (*LPP* 231–2)

Despite his wish not to be lionized it is difficult not to admire his attitude. We inhabit cultures of self-justification, blame and excuses; a man prepared to accept the consequences of his actions impresses us.

Dietrich Bonhoeffer's sense of responsibility and accountability was finely nuanced. In spite of his early affirmation of the centrality of the Church for theology and ethics, he did not feel accountable to the Confessing Church, which was in no position to know in full the magnitude of Nazi crimes and was therefore incapable of judging his actions. Neither did he feel accountable to the governing authorities represented by the court investigating his case, since the court was complicit in the crimes he resisted. Instead Bonhoeffer felt responsible to those unable to stand up for themselves who would suffer as the result of his inaction. Above all he felt himself to be responsible to God, who alone justifies. His prison poem 'Jonah' is surely an autobiographical echo of both his acceptance of judgement and his faith in God's power to justify sinners:

... My guilt must bear the wrath of God;
the righteous shall not perish with the sinner! (*LPP* 399)

The silence of the cross

Christian ethics is lived in the silence of the cross – a silence in which the believer is given responsibility for her actions. God's silence on the cross is not a silence of indifference, despair, or bewilderment: it is a silence of utter involvement and sheer passion. It is not an empty silence, for it addresses Christians in the Church community, in the commands of God and in the shaping of human character. Within the Church and for the world God calls the believer to the costly discipleship of the cross of Jesus Christ which reveals a '... divinity so odd/ He lets the Adam whom He made/ Perform the Acts of God'.[7] In the silence of the cross God both *takes* responsibility for the world and *gives* responsibility to those prepared to serve it. This twofold event creates the context for Christian ethics. It also provides the context in which Bonhoeffer's writings and actions may be evaluated. Only in the silence of the cross can we make sense of his exercise of moral responsibility – and of ours.

Notes

1   See *Dark Continent: Europe's Twentieth Century*, Mark Mazower, Penguin, 1998, p. xii. The whole book is a brilliant analysis of the 'story' of European democracy.

2   Letter to Paul Lehmann, 20 September 1941, cited in *Bonhoeffer: A Theology of Sociality*, Clifford J. Green, revised edition, Eerdmans, 1999, p. 346. The postwar history of Germany reveals just how wrong Bonhoeffer was in this prediction.

3   See, for example, Stanley Hauerwas 'The Church and Liberal Democracy: The Moral Limits of Secular Policy' in *A Community of Character*, University of Notre Dame Press, Indiana, 1981, pp. 72–86.

4   See *Development as Freedom*, Amartya Sen, OUP, 1999, in particular chapter 6.

5   Reinhold Niebuhr, 'The Death of a Martyr', *Christianity and Crisis*, 25, June 1945.

6   *After Virtue: a study in moral theory*, Alasdair MacIntyre, 2nd edition, Duckworth, 1985, p. 2. MacIntyre develops his argument in two subsequent books: *Whose Justice? Which Rationality?*, Duckworth, 1988; *Three Rival Versions of Moral Enquiry*, Duckworth, 1990.

7   For the source of the phrase 'a silence on the cross' and of these lines, see Chapter 1 for my discussion of the poem 'Friday's Child' by W.H. Auden.

Abbreviations and Bibliography

There is a bewildering quantity of publications by and about Dietrich Bonhoeffer. This section offers suggestions about where readers might look in order to explore Bonhoeffer's life and theology in greater depth. It incorporates abbreviations (abbreviations are printed in italics within brackets) for books referred to frequently.

Primary literature

Bonhoeffer's books, articles, lectures, sermons and letters are collected in their original language in the *Dietrich Bonhoeffer Werke*, published in Munich by Christian Kaiser Verlag (*DBWG*). There are 16 volumes (e.g. *DBWG 1*, *DBWG 2*, etc). A translation project is under way that will, in time, produce a complete English language version of the *Dietrich Bonhoeffer Works*; the publisher is Fortress Press, Minneapolis (DBW). The first volume appeared in 1996 and at the time of writing seven volumes of the *DBW* have been published:

Sanctorum Communio, Dietrich Bonhoeffer, Fortress Press, Minneapolis, 1998 *DBW 1*.

Act and Being, Dietrich Bonhoeffer, Fortress Press, Minneapolis, 1996, *DBW 2*.

Creation and Fall, Dietrich Bonhoeffer, Fortress Press, Minneapolis, 1997, *DBW 3*.

Discipleship, Dietrich Bonhoeffer [NB, the former English translation was titled *The Cost of Discipleship*], Fortress Press, Minneapolis, 2001, *DBW4*.

Life Together/Prayerbook of the Bible, Fortress Press, Minneapolis, 1996, *DBW 5*.
Fiction from Tegel Prison, Fortress Press, Minneapolis, 2000, *DBW 7*.
The Young Bonhoeffer 1918-1927, Fortress Press, Minneapolis, 2003, *DBW 9*.

The German edition includes a revised text based on a detailed re-examination of Bonhoeffer's manuscripts; an editor's introduction and postscript; extensive footnotes and, where a previous edition of a text exists, marginal references to the earlier edition. The English edition incorporates all of this, but with a new introduction by the editors of the English translation. There are additional footnotes explaining the translation and making any observations helpful to non-German-speaking readers, as well as marginal references to the pagination of the German edition to aid cross-referencing. Both the *DBWG* and the *DBW* are of high scholarly quality and will remain definitive long after *this* book has been forgotten.

Until the complete edition of the *Dietrich Bonhoeffer Works* is available, the following books are sound editions of Bonhoeffer's writings:
Christology, Dietrich Bonhoeffer (translated by Edwin Robertson) London, 1978 (*C*).
Ethics, Dietrich Bonhoeffer, SCM Press, London, 1963 edition (*E*).
Letters and Papers from Prison, Dietrich Bonhoeffer, SCM Press, London, 1984 (*LPP*).

Three volumes (edited and translated by Edwin Robertson) of Bonhoeffer's letters and papers are also useful sources, though now out of print.
No Rusty Swords, Dietrich Bonhoeffer, Collins, London, 1977 (*NRS*).
The Way to Freedom, Dietrich Bonhoeffer, Collins, London, 1972.
True Patriotism, Dietrich Bonhoeffer, Collins, London, 1973.

A good one volume collection of extracts from Bonhoeffer's writings is:
A Testament to Freedom: The Essential Writings of Dietrich Bonhoeffer, eds Geffrey B. Kelly and F. Burton Nelson, Harper Collins, 1991.

Nachlass Dietrich Bonhoeffer, eds D. Meyer and E. Bethge, Chr. Kaiser Verlag, Munich, 1987
Lists Bonhoeffer's manuscripts from his books, to every last fragmentary note, as well as all the books Bonhoeffer owned that survive.

Biographical sources

Eberhard Bethge's *Dietrich Bonhoeffer: A Biography*, Fortress Press, Minneapolis, 2000 (*DB*)
This new English translation restores sections omitted from previous English editions, updates the original text, corrects errors, and freshens up the earlier translation on which it is based. It is a *classic* of twentieth-century theology and the ultimate source of Bonhoeffer scholarship. Shorter biographies have been published but every serious student of twentieth-century theology should read Bethge's original study which takes the reader into the mind of a theologian and into the heart of theology.
    Dietrich Bonhoeffer: A Life in Pictures, E. Bethge, R. Bethge and C. Gremmels, SCM, London, 1986
A pictorial account of Bonhoeffer's life and of the events in which his life was set.
    I Knew Dietrich Bonhoeffer, eds W.-D. Zimmermann and R. G. Smith, Collins, London, 1973
Recollections of Bonhoeffer by some of those who knew him.

Bonhoeffer's theology

At the risk of appearing arrogant, it seems to me there are very few books on Bonhoeffer's theology that continue to be valuable beyond their initial print run! Here, I confine myself to books written or available in English.
The Theology of Dietrich Bonhoeffer, Ernst Feil, tr. Martin Rumscheidt, Fortress, Philadelphia, 1985
Argues for the continuity in Bonhoeffer's thought against some (e.g. Hanfried Müller) who suggested that Bonhoeffer's 'radical' later theology effected a decisive break from his earlier more traditional outlook.
    Reclaiming Dietrich Bonhoeffer: The Promise of his theology, Charles Marsh, Oxford University Press, 1994
Challenges the view that Bonhoeffer was philosophically casual and

intellectually superficial; an important interpretation, particularly of Bonhoeffer's early thought.

Many monographs on Bonhoeffer explore particular aspects of his theology, rather than attempting a general overview.
Bonhoeffer: A Theology of Sociality, Clifford J. Green (revised edition), Eerdmans, Grand Rapids, 1999
Focuses on Bonhoeffer's social theology.

Dietrich Bonhoeffer: Theologian of Reality, André Dumas, SCM, London, 1971
A deep, complex and quirky reading of Bonhoeffer through the lens of reality.

Karl Barth in the Theology of Dietrich Bonhoeffer, Andreas Pangritz, Eerdmans, Grand Rapids, 2000
Pangritz examines one of the crucial relationships of Bonhoeffer's life.

The Old Testament as the Book of Christ, Martin Kuske, Westminster, Philadelphia, 1976
A pellucid study of a single aspect of Bonhoeffer's theology that gives an example of what critical Bonhoeffer scholarship is like at its best.

Two books relate Bonhoeffer's legacy to contemporary challenges.

Dietrich Bonhoeffer: His Significance for North Americans, Larry Rasmussen, Fortress, Minneapolis, 1990

A Patriotism for Today: Love of Country in dialogue with the witness of Dietrich Bonhoeffer, Keith W. Clements, Collins, London, 1986.

Some of the best of Bonhoeffer scholarship has taken the form of essays.
The Cambridge Companion to Dietrich Bonhoeffer, edited by John W. de Gruchy, Cambridge University Press, 1999
Probably the best single volume on Bonhoeffer.

World Come of Age, edited by Ronald Gregor Smith, Collins, London, 1967
Contributors include Barth and Bultmann.

Individual essays on Bonhoeffer also appear 'hidden' away in books by theologians who are not 'Bonhoeffer specialists'; these are frequently more stimulating than essays by those who are 'expert' in the field.

'Dietrich Bonhoeffer' in *Word and Faith*, Gerhard Ebeling, SCM, London, 1963.

'Polyphonic Living: Dietrich Bonhoeffer' in *Self and Salvation*, David F. Ford, Cambridge University Press, 1999.

Bonhoeffer's ethics

Four studies have been important in helping me to understand Bonhoeffer's ethics, though I would not want to associate them with the deficiencies of this book. *Shaping the Future: The Ethics of Dietrich Bonhoeffer*, James Burtness, Fortress, Philadelphia, 1985; *Ethical Responsibility: Bonhoeffer's Legacy to the Churches*, eds John Godsey and Geffrey B. Kelly, Edwin Mellen Press, New York, 1981; *New Studies in Bonhoeffer's 'Ethics'*, ed. William J. Peck, Edwin Mellen Press, Lewiston, 1987; and *Bonhoeffer's Ethics: Old Europe and New Frontiers*, eds G. Carter *et al.*, Kok Pharos, Kampen, 1991.

The International Bonhoeffer Society (English Language Section) Newsletter annually updates the bibliography of publications on Bonhoeffer (details can be downloaded from the World Wide Web) and is one way to keep up to date with the rush of new books and articles that are following on the heels of the new edition.

Index